Eigentum des Landes Hessen
Gesamtschule Bischofsheim
Nr. VIII D2/74

Das Buch wird ausgeliehen an

Name	Klasse	von	bis	Zurück gegeben
Elvira Schmidt	6H	13.1.76		

How do you do   Stage Two

Edition B

Making Friends in London

Textbook with
Audio-Lingual
and Audio-Visual Course

Ferdinand Schöningh · Paderborn   42220

An English Audio-Lingual and Audio-Visual Course

Edition B Stage 2

Written and edited by:

Eric Orton, M.A.
Dr. Peter H. Stoldt

Harald Dolz
Oliver Goldfinch, M.A.
Norbert Hackethal
Hans-Roman Holzner, M.A.

Advisory Team:

Dr. Rudolf Höppner
Harald Maier
H. J. Schäfer
Ingvelde Schmidt-Reckert
Bernd Strecker
Werner Tauke
Prof. Dr. Günther Zimmermann

Redaktion:

Christof Hottenrott
John Stevens, B.A.
Gerald Williams, B.A.

Illustrated by:	Bildmaterial stellten zur Verfügung:
Kurt Schmischke	Camera Press, London Heinz Held, Köln London Transport

---

All rights reserved.
No part of this publication may be reproduced, stored in a retrieval system, or transmitted in any form or by any means, electronic, mechanical, photocopying, recording, or otherwise, without the prior permission of the Copyright owner.

© 1971 by Ferdinand Schöningh at Paderborn. Printed in Germany.

Herstellung: Ferdinand Schöningh, Paderborn. O.

ISBN 3 506 42220 0

CONTENTS

Unit	Texts, Games	Page	Structures, Tests
1	Step 1: (Audio-Lingual Material): A Television Advertisement Step 2: (Audio-Visual Material without text): A Special Offer (Audio-Visual Material with text): Step 3: Drills in Drill Book 2, unit 8 Step 4: Bob's Dinner Step 5: A tongue twister. A proverb. Rhymes Facts about Britain Step 6: Graded Material in Working with words and structures Additional Text: Roger the lion-tamer	8	Pam's hair is longer than Ann's hair. Eileen is as tall as Pam. Ann is not as tall as Eileen. My sister is the prettiest girl in the world. It's hot this morning, isn't it?
2	Step 1: A/L: The teacher's mistake Step 2: A/V: Tony has disappeared Step 3: Drills in DB 2, unit 9 Step 4: Hide and Seek Step 5: Can you solve this puzzle? Facts about Britain Step 6: Graded Material in WWWAS	16	I have just cleaned the board. I have had this dress since Friday. Have you had your holiday yet? He has just found the right answer. Where has Peter been all evening?
3	Step 1: A/L: You can't trust women! Step 2: A/V: England against Germany Step 3: Drills in DB 2, unit 10 Step 4: The Race Step 5: Facts about Britain At the Customs in Dover (A game with words) Step 6: Graded Material in WWWAS Additional Text: Kidnapped!	24	The postman has come. The runner has dropped the baton. How long have you been at home? Have you ever had a bad tooth? A test: Choose the right answer. See WWWAS
4	Step 1: A/L: Tony loves nut chocolate Step 2: A/V: The Crash Step 3: Drills in DB 2, unit 11 Step 4: Hit and Run Step 5: The Adverb Game The Farmer's Weather-Forecast Three Proverbs Facts about Britain Step 6: Graded Material in WWWAS Interpreting for Angelika	32	My sister draws badly. My friend sings well. He happily finishes his work. English children usually drink tea.

Unit	Texts, Games	Page	Structures, Tests

5	Step 1: A/L: Mother hated it!
	Step 2: A/V: Fire at school
	Step 3: Drills in DB 2, unit 12
	Step 4: Fire!
	Step 5: A funny rhyme
	        A Limerick
	        Facts about Britain
	Step 6: Graded Material in WWWAS
	        Additional Text: What a muddle!
		40	Were you tired yesterday?
			Tony had an egg, too.
			He replied a moment ago.

6	Step 1: A/L: The new Spring hat
	Step 2: A/V: A birthday present for Mrs. Hill
	Step 3: Drills in DB 2, unit 13
	Step 4: The latest hit
	Step 5: A Game: Word Chains
	        A Competition
	        Facts about Britain
	Step 6: Graded Material in WWWAS
		50	Did he like his present?
			Yesterday she didn't get up early.
			Didn't you help your mother? Yes, I did.
			Peter said: 'Please!'
			A word puzzle: see WWWAS

7	Step 1: A/L: At the Youth Club
	Step 2: A/V: Eiléen and Ann are in trouble
	Step 3: Drills in DB 2, unit 14
	Step 4: 'There's plenty of time!'
	Step 5: A Limerick
	        Facts about Britain
	        A Crossword Puzzle
	Step 6: Graded Material in WWWAS
	        Additional Text: The mail train crash
	        Monica's Diary
		58	Mr. Hill came round the corner.
			Ted sat down.
			May I go into the water?

8	Pictorial Introduction:
	        We are over London now.
	Step 1: A/V: The Harvest
	Step 2: A/L: A Holiday on the Farm
	Step 3: Drills in DB 3, unit 1
	Step 4: A letter from a farm
	Step 5: Sabine's English Phrase-Book
	        The 'Yes-No' Game
	Step 6: Graded Material in WWWAS
		69	Do you like eating eggs?
			Stop talking.
			Jill was able to ride.
			You mustn't forget.

9	Step 1: A/V: At the Greengrocer's
	Step 2: A/L: Shopping for a party
	Step 3: Drills in DB 3, unit 2
	Step 4: The party
	Step 5: Sabine's English Phrase-Book
	        Carsten's English Scrapbook
	        A Team Game: At the greengrocer's
	Step 6: Graded Material in WWWAS
	        Additional Text: Ben the big-head
		79	This shop is more expensive.
			She is the most beautiful girl.
			A house is more expensive than a flat.

Unit	Texts, Games	Page	Structures, Tests
10	Step 1: A/V: Burglars Step 2: A/L: Remember, remember, the fifth of November! Step 3: Drills in DB 3, unit 3 Step 4: A) November 5th 　　　　B) Lucky Jack Step 5: A Limerick 　　　　Carsten's English Scrapbook 　　　　Sabine's English Phrase-Book 　　　　A Spelling Game: Rockets and Jet Planes 　　　　English Customs Step 6: Graded Material in WWWAS	89	He is going to throw it. She wanted to but she couldn't. He ran to the party. He found a penny. He lit a firework.
11	Step 1: A/V: The Paper-Round Step 2: A/L: One pound fifty pence a week Step 3: Drills in DB 3, unit 4 Step 4: The paper-boy Step 5: Carsten's English Scrapbook 　　　　An Acting Game 　　　　Sabine's English Phrase-Book Step 6: Graded Material in WWWAS 　　　　Additional Text: The Woodpecker	99	I'll clean my bike by tomorrow. Shall I go to the butcher's? Yes, I'll have to work. How good is your English? A test in WWWAS
12	Step 1: A/V: Miss Peabody's bad memory Step 2: A/L: You won't forget, will you? Step 3: Drills in DB 3, unit 5 Step 4: Poor Miss Dinsdale! Step 5: Sabine's English Phrase-Book 　　　　English Customs 　　　　Peas 　　　　A Limerick 　　　　Carsten's English Scrapbook Step 6: Graded Material in WWWAS 　　　　Additional Text: Stop, thief!	109	No, I shan't go. You'll look after him, won't you? You drove well, didn't you?
13	Step 1: A/V: Westminster Step 2: A/L: Aren't your policemen wonderful! Step 3: Drills in DB 3, unit 6 Step 4: A) London's river 　　　　B) Sabine's diary Step 5: A game: The shopping-trip 　　　　Sabine's English Phrase-Book 　　　　Carsten's English Scrapbook 　　　　A Proverb 　　　　A Joke Step 6: Graded Material in WWWAS	119	Somebody has taken my bag. Nobody wants to take it. Each of you will need a raincoat. From whom did you get a book? Doreen has several new records. I have only a few pictures in my room. A test in WWWAS

Contents

Unit	Texts, Games	Page	Structures, Tests
14	Step 1: A/V: A bird called Esmeralda Step 2: A/L: Rubbish! Step 3: Drills in DB 3, unit 7 Step 4: 'Pretty Joe!' Step 5: Proverbs A guessing game Sabine's English Phrase-Book Step 6: Graded Material in WWWAS Additional Text: An exciting flight	129	Alan is bored because he has no fun. A book which will be useful. The old lady whose bird has gone. He thought, he flew, he paid. A postman is somebody who brings letters. A Test in WWWAS
15	Step 1: A/V: Stuck in a snowdrift Step 2: A/L: An exciting trip to hospital Step 3: Drills in DB 3, unit 8 Step 4: A) The newspaper report B) The reporter's story Step 5: We write a story A limerick A competition: True or False Sabine's English Phrase-Book Carsten's English Scrapbook English Customs Step 6: Graded Material in WWWAS Additional Text: Here is the news	139	Are there any eggs? There are some apples. Sorry, I haven't got any coffee. If I meet her, I'll tell her. Test Questions
16	Step 1: A/V: Going by tube Step 2: A/L: The Underground Step 3: Drills in DB 3, unit 9 Step 4: A Meal on a Tray Step 5: A Vocabulary Competition A Joke Sabine's English Phrase-Book Step 6: Graded Material in WWWAS Comprehension Dialogue	149	There isn't much food there. There were no good books there. He hasn't got much money. A little snow can be nice. Can you be an interpreter? Test your honesty
17	Step 1: A/V: A plane is on fire! Step 2: A/L: Good-byes at London Airport Step 3: Drills in DB 3, unit 10 Step 4: Sabine's Diary: Fasten your seat belts! Step 5: A Proverb Sabine's English Phrase-Book A Vocabulary Quiz-Game Step 6: Graded Material in WWWAS Additional Text: The Woodpecker; At Buckingham Palace Comprehension Dialogue Appendix: An English Christmas A Carol: I saw three ships	159	We all need a rest. She is afraid of flying. He left without saying good-bye. We waited all day, although the weather was bad. Pattern Practice Tests in WWWAS

Unit 1

Step 1

A conversation: A television advertisement

Reporter: Tell me, Mrs. Bloggs, that is your washing on that table, isn't it?
Mrs. Bloggs: Yes, it is.
Reporter: And you can see the Pimo shirts on this table, can't you?
Mrs. Bloggs: Yes, I can.
Reporter: Now, Mrs. Bloggs, the Pimo shirts are whiter than your shirts, aren't they?
Mrs. Bloggs: Yes, of course. You're quite right. They are whiter and cleaner.
Reporter: Do you use Pimo for your washing?
Mrs. Bloggs: No, I don't. But I must get Pimo at once. Look lovelier with Pimo shirts.
Reporter: Yes, you too can have the whitest washing in your street. Buy Pimo. Pimo is cheaper. Pimo packets are bigger. Pimo is the best. Pimo!

Step 2

A special offer

3

4

5

6

7

8

Unit 1

Unit 1

a) Look and listen
b) Look, listen and repeat

A special offer

Speaker:
1 Bob is a very large and lively dog. | He needs plenty of food.

Ann:
2 And then I need two tins of meaty dog food. |

Shop assistant:
This new food is very tasty. | It's our special offer this week.

Ann:
3 What is this special offer?

Shop assistant:
You get three tins for the price of two, | and a plastic bone.

Ann:
4 That's a wonderful offer. | Please, put nine tins into my suitcase.

Ann:
5 Look, Mummy, aren't I clever? | This new dog food is as good as the best meat. | And it makes dogs healthy.

Mrs. Hill:
6 But do we need nine tins?

Ann:
Ah, they are a special offer this week, | three for the price of two. Isn't it exciting?

Ann:
7 Oh dear, Bob doesn't like the new food.
Mrs. Hill:
He's barking. He hates this meat.

Mrs. Hill:
8 Bob doesn't like the plastic bone. | I don't think this special offer is so wonderful.

Questions and answers

1. What does a large dog need?
2. Is the new dog food fishy?
3. How many tins can you get for the price of two?
4. Where is the assistant putting the nine tins?
5. How good is the new dog food?
6. What is exciting?
7. Why is Bob barking?
8. What does Bob think of the plastic bone?

Drills in Drill Book 2, Unit 8

Step 3

Bob's dinner

Step 4

A man with a large suitcase is standing at the door of number 2, Beech Lane. Mrs. Hill opens the door.
"Good morning, madam," the man says. "Do you own a dog?"
"Yes, we do," replies Mrs. Hill.
"Good! Then I have exciting news for you! I am the WUFF-WUFF man!"
"Who?"
"The WUFF-WUFF man!"
"Oh? And who is he?"

"Good heavens, madam! Don't you know? WUFF-WUFF is the newest, tastiest, meatiest dog food in the world! Everybody is talking about it! It makes your dog happier and livelier than your neighbours' dogs! It is as good as your best Sunday dinner! It is in a bigger tin and with it you get a wonderful special offer!"
"We have plenty of dog food, thank you. Good morning."
"But madam — the special offer! You can, for the next two weeks, buy three tins of WUFF-WUFF for the price of two — AND, with every three tins your dog gets a meat-flavoured plastic bone! FREE!!"
"No thank you! Now please go!"
"You can buy just one tin, madam, can't you? Think of it, madam! WUFF-WUFF can make your dog cleverer, younger than ....."

Unit 1

20 "Bob!" calls Mrs. Hill. "It's time for your dinner."
". . . . . Is that your d-dog, madam? He is a large dog, isn't he? He looks very l-lively and f-fierce, doesn't he? Yes — well, I must go now. G-g-good morning, madam."
"Come on, Bob," laughs Mrs. Hill.
25 "Wuff-wuff," barks Bob.

Step 5 1 We write a scene and act it

A man with a big suitcase comes to Mrs. Black's house. It is four o'clock in the afternoon, and Mrs. Black has no time. But the man says: "I'm the Puss-Puss Man." He is selling big tins of Puss-Puss, a new cat food. The fish in these tins is tastier and better and cheaper. It's the best cat food in the world. It is as good as fresh fish. But Mrs. Black's cat doesn't like fish. The man goes on. He has a special offer. Three plastic roses for every tin of cat food. Mrs. Black says: "We have plenty of roses in our garden." A big wild dog rushes into Mrs. Black's front-garden. "Is that your dog?" the man asks. "It's my neighbour's dog, Bob," Mrs. Black replies. The man says he must go.

Now write the dialogue. Begin with: Man: "Good afternoon!"

2 Comparisons

Mrs. Dean's car is old.

Mr. Hill's car is **older**.

Mr. Black's car is **the oldest**.

Pam's hair is longer **than** Eileen's hair. Ann's hair is shorter **than** Eileen's hair. Eileen is **as** tall **as** Pam, but Ann is **not as** tall **as** Eileen.

3 Compare these bikes

 This bike is new**er than** that bike.
Go on with: dear, fast, long, high, small, old, cheap.

4 We find the right adjectives and complete these sentences

> Hair is longer than grass
> (young, rich, old, tall, long, warm, cold)

a) Summer is ..... winter.

b) Winter is ..... summer.

c) In summer the days are ..... in winter.

d) Dentists are ..... postmen.

e) Men are ..... boys.

f) Girls are .... women.

g) Grandfathers are ..... grandsons.

5 Copy and complete with 'bigger' or 'smaller'

a) London is ..... than Birmingham.

b) Bonn is ..... than London.

c) A goldfish is ..... than a cat.

d) A bus is ..... than a car.

e) A flower is ..... than a tree.

6 We form sentences

a)

My mother My sister My friend My father My brother Our neighbour	is the	nicest prettiest happiest naughtiest funniest luckiest laziest fattest best sweetest	woman man girl boy person	in the world.

b) Now sell a house to the pupil beside you. Explain: This is the ..... house in the street. It has the ..... garden and the ..... garage. The trees have the ..... apples. (Use the superlatives of: pretty, good, big, sweet.)

7 We copy and complete ●

8 We compare the pupils in this class and write sentences about them

Mary Peter John Ann Susan Philip Andrew Michael Caroline	is isn't	as as	tall small fat thin clever silly late for school hungry	as	Eric Ursula Fred Marion Karen Roger Charles Edward

9 Copy and complete with comparisons ●

10 We talk about the weather

It's	hot cold wet fine foggy white	this morning, today, this spring, this summer, this autumn, this winter,	isn't it?

We answer: "Yes, it is, *or* No, it isn't."

11 Please change the sentences, but don't change their meaning ■

12 Not so very important ★

13 Who can read this tongue-twister in the shortest time?

> Don't walk in this wet and windy weather, Walter!

Read it three times. For every mistake add five seconds to your time.

14 A proverb
Better late than never!

15 Rhymes

| As cold as ice, | As pretty as a flower, | As white as milk, |
| As quick as mice. | As high as a tower. | As soft as silk. |

As tired as a dog,   As sweet as honey,
As thick as fog.   As scarce as money.

Make a rhyming pair with these words: ball, round, hall, big.

16 Facts about Britain

Britain's highest mountain is Ben Nevis in Scotland.
It is 4,406 feet high. One foot = 30.5 cm.

Unit 2

Step 1

A conversation: The teacher's mistake

Teacher: Read the next sentence, Ted.
Eric: Ted hasn't arrived yet, sir.
Jean: Perhaps he's forgotten the time.
Teacher: Perhaps he's ill.
Bill: No, sir, I've seen him outside the headmaster's room.
(Ted comes in)

Teacher: Where have you been, Ted? You're late again. I'm very angry.
Ted: I'm sorry, sir. I've just come from the headmaster.
Teacher: And what's he said to you?
Ted: He's thanked me.
Teacher: Good heavens!
Ted: I've found fifty pence on the floor of the school hall —
the headmaster's fifty pence!

Step 2

Tony has disappeared

3

4

5

6

7

8

Unit 2

Unit 2

a) Look and listen
b) Look, listen and repeat

Tony has disappeared

1

2

3

4

5

6

7

8

Speaker:
1 The Hill family are watching television.

Mrs. Hill:
Well, that's the end of the film. Where is Tony?

Ann:
2 He's not in the dining-room. There's no sign of him. | I haven't seen him since seven o'clock.

Mrs. Hill:
3 Look for him outside, Peter, and try the neighbours.

Peter:
4 I'm doing my best, but I can't find him. | Nobody knows where he is.

Mrs. Hill:
5 Please get the car out, Tom, and search the district.

Ann:
6 Perhaps there's been an accident!

Peter:
7 Perhaps he's in London and has lost his way.

Speaker:
8 Ann comes back into the room.

Ann:
Tony hasn't disappeared. | I've discovered him upstairs. He's in bed!

Questions and answers

1 What are the Hill family doing?
2 Can Ann see Tony?
3 Where must Peter look for Tony?
4 Do the neighbours know where Tony is?
5 Must Mr. Hill search the house?
6 What does Ann think?
7 What does Peter think?
8 Where has Ann discovered Tony?

Drills in Drill Book 2, Unit 9

`Step 3`

Hide and Seek

`Step 4`

Mrs. Hill: Have you seen the dog, Peter? I haven't seen him since six o'clock.
Peter: No, Mum, I've been upstairs all evening.
Mrs. Hill: Have you seen him, Tony?
Tony: No, Mummy.   5
Mrs. Hill: Have you, Ann?
Ann: No, Mummy, I've shouted for him and I've tried all the neighbours. Nobody has seen him.
Mrs. Hill: Oh well, dear, you've done your best. Ah! Your father has just 10 come in — perhaps he has seen Bob.
Ann: Daddy — have you found Bob?
Mr. Hill: No. Why — has he disappeared?
Tony: Yes, there hasn't been a sign of him for almost three hours.
Peter: We must search the district, Dad.   15
Tony: Take the car, Daddy.
Ann: Please, Daddy! Perhaps he has . . . . .
Mr. Hill: All right, all right! Give me a chance! I must get the car out first!
Mr. Hill: Betty, we've found Bob! He's been in the garage all evening! 20 Silly old dog!

Unit 2

Mrs. Hill: Oh good! But where has Peter gone?
Tony: He's gone out on his bike.
Mrs. Hill: What! At this time of night! Perhaps he has lost his way or had an accident!
Mr. Hill: Don't be silly, Betty. Of course he hasn't.
Mrs. Hill: Well, do something! Don't just stand there! Telephone the police-station! Ask the neighbours! Oh, dear, oh dear!
Peter: Hallo, Mum! Where has Dad gone?
Mrs. Hill: Peter! Where have you been? We have looked for you everywhere.
Peter: And I've searched everywhere for Bob, but I haven't found him.
Mrs. Hill: Why, hasn't Tony told you? Your father has discovered him in the garage.
Peter: Oh! Good! But where has Dad just gone?
Mrs. Hill: Where has . . . . . ? Oh no! Now someone else has disappeared!

Step 5 **1 We answer the questions**

a) Where has Peter been all evening?
b) Who has disappeared?
c) Has Bob gone to the neighbours?
d) Where has Bob been all evening?
e) Has Peter gone out in the car?
f) Has Peter had an accident?
g) Has Mr. Hill telephoned the school?
h) Who else has disappeared?

2 We find the questions

Answer:	I have just returned from school.
Question:	Have you just returned from school?

a) I have cleaned my teeth.
b) I have washed my hands.
c) I have packed my school bag.
d) I haven't been late for school.
e) I have answered ten questions at school.
f) I have had my lunch.
g) I have come back home at half past four.
h) I have done my homework.
i) I have watched television.
j) I have gone to bed.

3 I have already done it!

I You We They	have	already	copied the sentences. finished the dictation. seen these pictures. written ten sentences.
He She My neighbour	has	just	read this story. completed my work. got out my books. cleaned the board. found the questions. found the right answer.

4 Tony is bored

Put in Tony's answers and use
the right tense with "just".

Mrs. Hill: Don't watch television so early in the afternoon, Tony.
　　　　　　Do your homework.
Tony: I have just done it, Mummy.
Mrs. Hill: Then clean your shoes.
Tony: I have .....
Mrs. Hill: Go into the garden.

Unit 2

Tony: I have . . . . .
Mrs. Hill: Have a bath. Finish your book. Read the evening paper. Telephone your girl-friend. Wash Daddy's car. Write a letter.

5 We read

[t]   I have ask**ed** the neighbours, search**ed** and look**ed** for Bob everywhere.

[d]   Peter has disappear**ed**, and I have telephon**ed** the police.

[id] I've shout**ed** and shout**ed**.

6 Girls and their clothes

We answer these questions and use "since"

Joan: I like your skirt. How long have you had it?
Pam: I have had it **since** Friday.
Joan: That is a nice blouse. How long have you had it?
Pam: (last Thursday)
Joan: That is a pretty dress. How long have you had it?
Pam: (Christmas)
Joan: That is a beautiful hat, lovely coat, wonderful pullover, pretty belt, nice tie, beautiful swim-suit.
Pam: (last year, last summer, last month, last spring)

7 Where have you been? ●

8 We give classroom orders and say what we have just done ●

9 Give short answers to the following questions ■

10 Complete the report of "Hide and Seek" ★

11 Can you solve this puzzle?
What are these rooms?
 a) TICKENH   b) BROOMED   c) GNIDIN-MORO

22   Unit 2

12 Facts about Britain

The average British woman is 5 feet 3 inches high.
(1 inch = 25.4 millimetres) (1 stone = 14 pounds. 1 pound = 0,453 kg)
The average British woman weighs 9 stones 10 pounds.

Unit 2

Unit 3

Step 1   **A conversation: You can't trust women!**

Tony: You look very unhappy. What's the matter?
Peter: I can't find my pen.
Tony: Have you looked in your school bag?
Peter: I've just looked. My pen isn't there.
Tony: Then search your room.
Peter: I've already searched it.
Tony: Haven't you written a letter with it this afternoon?
Peter: Yes, I have. But now it has disappeared, and I must finish my homework.
Tony: Ask Ann. Perhaps she's found it.
Peter: Yewhooo! Ann! Have you seen my pen?
Ann: Oh, sorry, Peter! I've just borrowed it. I've taken it out of your bag. I can't find my pen and I must start my homework.
Tony and Peter: You can't trust women!

Step 2   **England against Germany**

Unit 3

England against Germany

Look and listen
Look, listen and repeat

Television-commentator:

1. Now there is the last race of the big athletics match — | the 4 × 440 yards relay.

2. England and Germany have the same score.

3. Here comes the starter. | He fires his gun, and they're off!

4. And now, at the end of the first lap, Germany has taken the lead!

5. The start of the third lap, | and now the English runner Ellis is at Schmidt's shoulder | and is overtaking him.

6. The end of the third lap. | Ellis is giving the baton to the fourth runner. | No! he has dropped the baton.

7. The German runner Kuschke has taken the lead. | The German visitors are jumping up and down with excitement.

8. Twenty yards from the finish. | Kuschke races to the finish. | Germany has won the race, and the match.

26 Unit 3

Questions and answers

1. What is the last race?
2. Who has the same score?
3. Who fires the gun?
4. When does Germany take the lead?
5. What is the name of the English runner?
6. When does Ellis give the baton to the fourth runner?
7. Who has taken the lead?
8. Who races to the finish?

Drills in Drill Book 2, Unit 10

Step 3

Step 4

The race

March in England is often wet and cold. Nonetheless many English schools have their athletics match in March, at the end of the Spring Term. Peter's school in Wood Green always has an athletics match against the school in Tottenham on the third Wednesday in March, and today is the day of the match. The runners are now ready for the last race, the 4 × 440 yards relay. Both schools have the same score, and so the result of this race is very important.
The starter fires his gun — and they are off!

It has been a very exciting race: so far first one school and then the other has led. Now the third lap has started, and the runner from Peter's school has taken the lead. By the end of the lap he has increased his lead to ten yards. Now he has given the baton to the fourth runner. No! He hasn't! He has dropped it! The Tottenham runner has overtaken him!

Two hundred yards from the finish, and still the Tottenham runner is leading, but the Wood Green runner is now only two yards behind him. Everybody is shouting, and Peter and his friends are jumping up and down with excitement. Fifty yards, and now the Wood Green runner is at the Tottenham boy's shoulder. Ten yards from the finish — and he has taken the lead! Only inches in front, he races to the finish — and Peter's school has won the race, and the match!

Step 5 **1 We answer these questions**

    a) When is the day of the match?
    b) What is the last race?
    c) Who fires the gun?
    d) Who takes the lead in the third lap?
    e) How big is his lead by the end of the third lap?
    f) Has the Tottenham runner dropped his baton, too?
    g) Is the Wood Green runner leading two hundred yards from the finish?
    h) When does the Wood Green runner take the lead?
    i) Who has won the match?

2 Correct these silly sentences

A	B
The cat	has just dropped the baton.

Mother	has just asked for a box of chalk.
The postman	has just brought a dozen eggs.
The runner	has just given me a pound of sausages.
The farmer	has just jumped into the basket.
The teacher	has just made a cake.
The shop assistant	has just come with our letters.

3 I have already done it, Mummy ●

4 Spring cleaning

We choose the right past participle from this list for each sentence:
taken, cleaned, seen, washed, got up, made, dried

a) It's half past seven. Have you . . . . ., Ann?
b) Have you . . . . . your bed, Peter? I must clean your room now.
c) Have you . . . . . the cups and plates, Tony? Then go out and buy some soap-powder.
d) Have you already . . . . . the bathroom curtains, Mummy?
e) Have you . . . . . the books out of the living-room, Daddy?
f) Have you . . . . . the windows in the dining-room, Ann?
g) Have you . . . . . the dirty floor in Peter's room, Mummy?

5 We write many questions

How long	have you has your brother has your friend has your mother	been	at school? at home? in the garden? in bed? in the living-room?

Then answer the questions. For example: I have been at home **since** one o'clock.

6 Not yet

Has Tony got up yet?
No, he hasn't got up yet.

a) Has Peter eaten his breakfast yet?
b) Has Ann drunk her tea yet?

c) Has Daddy gone to work yet?
d) Has the teacher arrived yet?
e) Has the bell rung yet?
f) Has Peter done his homework yet?
g) Has the television programme begun yet?
h) Has the dog had his walk yet?

7 Haven't you yet?

> Have you started your homework?
> **Haven't you** started your homework **yet**?

a) Have you finished your homework?
b) Have you given the book to your neighbour?
c) Have you found my pen?
d) Has your friend taken your advice?
e) Has your brother seen this film?
f) Has your sister come back?
g) Has your uncle gone upstairs?
h) Have you washed?

8 Ever-Never ●

9 The professor loses his way

(Look at the pictures and tell the story) ⟶

1 Today is the day of the football . . . . . England a . . . . . Germany. Professor Bloggs is g . . . . . to the b . . . . .
2 The bus a . . . . ., and the . . . . . climbs u . . . . .
3 The professor o . . . . . his book.
4 The time is . . . . ., and the . . . . . has already s . . . . .
5 The professor is still . . . . . The book must be very i . . . . . The . . . . . stops and e . . . . . climbs out. The time is . . . . .
6 The professor has at last f . . . . . his . . . . . He h . . . . . to a café and w . . . . the match on t . . . . . All's w . . . . .
7 England has w . . . . . the . . . . . Ev . . . . . is j . . . . . up and down with . . . . .

10 Can you add the verbs? ■

11 Choose the right answer ★

12 Facts about Britain

Shops in Britain don't open until nine o'clock and they close at half past five in the afternoon.

13 At the Customs in Dover (A game with words)

Customs Officer: Good morning, sir. Is that your suitcase?
German tourist: Yes, it is.
Customs Officer: Where have you come from, sir?
German tourist: I have come from Wuppertal.
Customs Officer: And what have you got in your suitcase?
Pupil tourist 1: I've got one white shirt in my suitcase.
Pupil tourist 2: I've got one white shirt and three books in my suitcase.
Pupil tourist 3: I've got one white shirt, three books and . . . . .

Go on!

Unit 3

Unit 4

Step 1   **A conversation: Tony loves nut chocolate**

Mrs. Hill: You're eating very slowly, Tony.
Don't you like your Irish Stew?
Tony: Of course I do.
Ann: You've cooked it beautifully, Mummy.
Mrs. Hill: Don't eat so quickly, Peter. There's enough stew for everybody.
Peter: You're looking very sadly at your potatoes, Tony.
Tony: I can't eat them.
Mrs. Hill: But you usually eat six potatoes for lunch.
Mr. Hill: Pass the stew please, Peter. Pass it carefully, please.
I don't want it on my trousers!
Mrs. Hill: Where are you going, Tony?
Tony: I'm sorry, Mummy. I don't feel well.
Mrs. Hill: He's never eaten so badly. I can't understand it.
Ann: I can. He's eaten half a pound of nut chocolate this morning!

Step 2   **The crash**

Unit 4

Unit 4

The crash

Look and listen
Look, listen and repeat

Speaker:

1 Peter is on his journey home. | The road is wet, and there is a lot of traffic on it.

2 Peter turns left and stops at the traffic-lights.

3 Now a fast car is overtaking Peter. Suddenly he sees a car in front of them. It is on the wrong side of the road.

4 Peter stops quickly, and the car behind him stops, too. | But the car hits the back of Peter's bike.

5 There is a loud crash, and Peter falls off his bike.

6 Peter is O.K. | He is looking at the big dent in the back of his bike.

7 The driver of the car says to Peter:

Driver:
I'm very sorry. It's my fault.

8 *Driver:*
Here's three pounds for the cost of the repair.

Questions and answers

1 Where is Peter going?
2 Where does Peter turn?
3 Who is overtaking Peter?
4 What does Peter do?
5 What does Peter do?
6 Is Peter's bike all right?
7 Was the crash Peter's fault?
8 How much is the repair?

Drills in Drill Book 2, Unit 11

Step 3

Step 4

Hit and Run

It has been the first fine Sunday of the year. The Hills — and thousands of other families — have been to the coast for the day. On the journey home the traffic moves very slowly. It is raining, and the children are tired.
"I'm hungry," says Tony.
Nobody answers him.
"I'm hungry!" Tony shouts.

5

"Be quiet!" his father **angrily replies**.
They slowly move two or three yards, and then they stop again.
"Look, Tom," says Mrs. Hill — "we can turn left after two hundred yards and get home by a different road. There isn't usually much traffic on it."
Soon they are driving happily along empty roads. Mr. Hill lights his pipe, and Mrs. Hill gives the children some chocolate. Suddenly a small red car appears in front of them — it is on the wrong side of the road, and it is moving very fast. Mr. Hill stops quickly — but the road is wet! The car hits a tree! Mr. Hill is very angry. There is a big dent in the back of his car, and the other car is quickly disappearing. Mr. Hill thinks sadly of the cost of the repair.
Two miles to Wood Green and home. It is still raining, and everybody is unhappy. They stop at the **traffic-lights**. There is a crash. A Rolls Royce has hit them and has damaged the back of the car even more. "I'm awfully sorry," says the gentleman in the big **car to** Mr. Hill. "It's my fault, I know, and the damage looks quite bad. Here is **a** hundred pounds. I'm sorry, but I can't stop. Good-bye, sir."
"Well, well," says Mr. Hill.
"You're a very lucky man, aren't you?" says Mrs. Hill.

Step 5 **1** **We answer these questions**

    a) How does the traffic move?
    b) Is it raining hard?
    c) Are the Hills on a journey to the coast?
    d) How is Mr. Hill driving along the empty roads?
    e) On which side of the road does the small red car appear?
    f) What does Mr. Hill's **car hit**?
    g) Does the driver of the small **red** car stop?
    h) Where does the second **car** hit Mr. Hill's **car**?
    i) Why is Mr. Hill a lucky man?

2 **Pam's dancing lesson**

Pam is a very good dancer.	She dances **well**.
Pam's friend Jack is a bad dancer.	He dances bad**ly**.
Jack is very slow.	He walks slow**ly**.
Pam is quick.	She walks quick**ly**.
Pam is careful.	She dresses careful**ly**.
Jack is untidy.	He dresses untid**ily**.
Pam is gent**le**.	She gent**ly** takes Jack's hand.

Now ask your left neighbour questions: How does Pam dance?
How does Jack walk? How do you dress? How does your father dance?
How does your mother drive? Can you swim well? Can you write well?

3 Describe six people. Then ask the pupil beside you questions.

My friend	speaks	very well.
The pupil on my left	eats	very badly.
The pupil on my right	writes	too quickly.
My sister	draws	too slowly.
My neighbour's son	sings	loudly.
My dentist's daughter	laughs	softly.
		nicely.

4 Peter's report ●

5 What's right?

English children		drink coffee.
German children		drink tea.
British girls	usually	have black bread.
German boys		have white bread.
London women		wear school ties.
Bonn men		don't wear school hats.
		start school at eight.
		begin school at nine.

6 Complete

We pick one of these adjectives for each sentence and make it into an adverb:
(quick, kind, happy, unhappy, bad, sudden, quiet, careful)

a) Peter ..... finishes his lunch.
b) He ..... runs to the bus stop.

Unit 4

c) He ..... helps an old woman on to the bus.
d) The bus starts .....
e) The old woman falls .....
f) She cries .....
g) Peter ..... helps her.

7   Where have you been? ●

8   Find the opposites

silently, slowly, well, wrongly, unhappily.
to appear, to hate, to lose, to stop, to get up.

9   Complete ■

10   Betty is very naughty. Interpreting for Angelika ★

11   The adverb game

We divide into two teams.

The first member of team A says a simple sentence: "My friend works."
The first member of team B must now repeat this sentence and add an adverb:
"My friend works well."
One pupil is the referee and gives minus points for pronunciation mistakes,
and for pupils who can't think of a sentence or an adverb.

12   The farmers' weather-forecast

Red sky in the morning,   Red sky at night,
Shepherd's warning.   Shepherd's delight.

13   Three proverbs

Don't throw away the baby with the bathwater.
You can't have your cake and eat it.
You can't teach an old dog new tricks.

14   Facts about Britain

People live very closely together in England: 800 people per square mile —
that is nine times as many as in the U.S.A. but not as many as in Germany.

Unit 5

Step 1   A conversation: Mother hated it!

Mrs. Black: Hallo, Ann! How is your mother today?
Ann: She's quite well again. But she was ill in bed yesterday. Daddy telephoned the doctor, and he said Mummy must have a day in bed. She hated it!
Mrs. Black: Oh dear, I'm very sorry. But who cooked your lunch?
Ann: Grandmother invited us, and we had a beautiful lunch at her house.
Mrs. Black: And who cleaned your house?
Ann: Oh, Daddy cleaned the bedrooms, and I helped.
Mrs. Black: And your brothers?
Ann: They worked in the garden.
Mrs. Black: But who cooked your supper, dear?
Ann: Tony discovered cold meat and tomatoes in the larder, and we also had a nice cup of tea. Then we all washed up.
Mrs. Black: Were you very tired at the end of that day?
Ann: Oh no! But Mummy was! She shouted orders all day.

Step 2   Fire at school

Unit 5

Look and listen
Look, listen and repeat

Fire at school

Speaker:
1 Tony's school is playing football against Tottenham. | Suddenly Mr. Dean notices a lot of smoke.

2 He fetches another teacher. | Then they rush back to the school.

3 The headmaster's house is on fire | and there is a big crowd in the road.

4 *A policeman:*
I have already telephoned the fire-brigade.

Mr. Dean:
5 I must get the school reports!

Speaker:
Mr. Dean rushes into the house.

Speaker:
6 Two minutes later the fire-brigade arrives. | One fireman climbs the ladder. | Three others look for Mr. Dean.

7 The crowd is watching and waiting. | At last the firemen appear again. | They have Mr. Dean with them, but not the school reports.

8 One minute later the house crashes to the ground, | but Mr. Dean is safe and sound.

Questions and answers

1 Is Tony's school playing for Tottenham?
2 Who rushes back?
3 Whose house is on fire?
4 Who has telephoned?
5 What is Mr. Dean getting?
6 When does the fire-brigade arrive?
7 What is the crowd doing?
8 When does the house crash to the ground?

Drills in Drill Book 2, Unit 12

Step 3

Step 4

Fire!

The fire at number three, Beech Lane, started in the living-room. Something frightened old Mrs. Naish's cat; the cat jumped out of its chair and knocked over the electric fire.
Peter noticed the smoke first. He quickly fetched his father, and Mr. Hill at once telephoned the fire-brigade. Then he, Mrs. Hill and the children hurried across the road to Mrs. Naish's garden. The whole living-room of the house was now in flames, and the kitchen and hall were also on fire. They all called, but there was no answer from Mrs. Naish.

The fire-brigade — and the police — arrived three minutes later, but now almost the whole house was on fire. There was a big crowd in the road, and

policemen and firemen were everywhere. One fireman climbed a ladder, and another looked for Mrs. Naish; two little boys laughed with excitement.
"Look! Look at the roof! Mrs. Naish's cat!" Ann suddenly shouted.
There was a loud scream, and an old lady rushed into the house.
5 "Who was that? Stop! Stop!" called a policeman.
"That was Mrs. Naish," answered somebody in the crowd: "she returned from the shops a minute ago."

Three firemen disappeared into the house. Minute followed minute, and the crowd in the road watched and waited. At last the firemen appeared again —
10 and they had Mrs. Naish with them. Minutes later the whole house crashed to the ground.

"Oh, my cat — my poor little cat!" cried old Mrs. Naish.
Then Bob noticed something. He rushed into the garden of number five, next-door to Mrs. Naish's, and barked. He barked again — and again. Every-
15 body looked, and there, on the roof of number five, was Mrs. Naish's cat — safe and sound!
Houses have only one life — but cats have nine!

Step 5 **1 Questions**

a) Who noticed the smoke first?
b) Who called the fire-brigade?
c) Was there an answer from Mrs. Naish?
d) Who watched and waited in the road?
e) How many firemen disappeared into the house?
f) Who first noticed the cat next-door?

2 Today   **Yesterday**

I am happy.   I **was** happy, too.
You are sad.   You **were** sad, too.
The teacher is angry.   The teacher **was** angry, too.
We are late.   We **were** late, too.
You are naughty.   You **were** naughty, too.
The children are tired. The children **were** tired, too.

Were you Was your father Were your parents Was your friend Were you and your sister	sleepy sad angry late tired unhappy lucky	this morning? an hour ago? yesterday afternoon?

Ask your neighbour questions. He can answer with:

"Yes, I was" or "No, I wasn't".
"Yes, he was" or "No, he wasn't".
"Yes, they were" or "No, they weren't".
"Yes, we were" or "No, we weren't".

3 **Every morning** **Yesterday morning**

I have tea. I **had** tea, too.
You have coffee. You **had** coffee, too.
Tony has an egg. Tony **had** an egg, too.
We have toast. We **had** toast, too.
You have sausages. You **had** sausages, too.
They have cornflakes. They **had** cornflakes, too.

4 My breakfast yesterday morning was very nice.

I had . . . . .

My mother . . .

My father . . . . .

Our dog . . . . .

5 A wonderful birthday tea

Yesterday was Sheila's birthday. She invited Ann, and they had a wonderful tea. There was a big birthday cake on the table, and beside each plate there was a small box of chocolates. There were sandwiches, cream buns and biscuits, and there was lemonade or tea. There were ten girls at the table. After tea they all had ices in the garden, and everybody had a very nice afternoon.

Now we answer these questions with "Yes, there was (were)" or "No, there wasn't (weren't)"

Was there a big cake? Was there a cat on the table?
Was there lemonade on the table? Were there apples on the table?
Was there a box beside Ann's plate? Were there ten girls at Sheila's house?

6 There was *or* there were? ●

7 We pronounce carefully

[d]	[t]
I arrived	I searched
you called	you fetched
he returned	he barked
we telephoned	we looked
you answered	you jumped
they listened	they laughed

8 We read: [t] or [d]?

The cat appeared on the roof and jumped.
The policemen arrived and searched the house.
The fireman climbed a ladder and fetched the cat.

9 We remember:

to hurry:	he hurries today	and he hurried yesterday.
to reply:	he replies	— he replied
to drop:	he drops it	— he dropped it a moment ago.

10 At the dance

Today Pam and Jack are at a dance.
The music is very lively.
They watch the other people.
They start a Quick Foxtrot.
They have an ice at the bar.
They talk about their holiday.
Jack pays for the ices.
They return from the dance at a quarter to ten.

Last week they were at a dance, too.
Last week . . . . .

11 Where was it a moment ago?

Pupil 1: Look at my desk. There is a book on it. Pick up that book. What have you just done?
Pupil 2: I have picked up your book.
Pupil 1: And where is the book now?
Pupil 2: It's on my desk.
Pupil 1: And where was it a moment ago?
Pupil 2: It was on your desk.

Now we repeat this conversation with: exercise-book, pencil, ruler, pen.

Pupil 1: Eric, go to the door and open it. Thank you, sit down.
John, who opened the door a moment ago?
Pupil 2: Eric opened it.
Pupil 1: Fred, clean the board. Peter, touch my desk. Ann, close the window.

12 The dog was safe and sound

We write down this story:

Yesterday Mr. Hill (to start) the car and (to turn) left round the corner. Suddenly a dog (to appear), (to rush) into the middle of the road and (to bark). There (to be) a cat on the other side.
Mr. Hill's car (to touch) the dog, but it (to be) all right and (to hurry) into the nearest house. Mr. Hill (to sigh). This (to be) his lucky day.

Unit 5

13 Did Bob lose his way? ■

14 You are a newspaper reporter ★

15 A funny rhyme: A Limerick

There was an old man with a beard,
Who said, "It is just as I feared!
Two owls and a hen,
Four larks and a wren
Have all built their nests in my beard!"

16 Facts about Britain

Two households in five have a washing machine.

One household in three has a refrigerator

Three households in four have a vacuum cleaner,

and four in five a television set.

Unit 5

Unit 6

Step 1

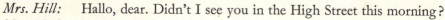

A conversation: The new spring hat

Mrs. Hill:	Hallo, dear. Didn't I see you in the High Street this morning?
Mrs. Black:	Yes, you did.
Mrs. Hill:	And since when have you had that hat?
Mrs. Black:	I've had it since this morning, dear. I needed a new spring hat.
Mrs. Hill:	Did you buy it at Mrs. Newman's shop?
Mrs. Black:	No, I didn't. The new shop beside it is much better.
Mrs. Hill:	And did you see many nice hats?
Mrs. Black:	Yes, I did. Do you like this hat?
Mrs. Hill:	I don't like those red flowers at the back.
Mrs. Black:	What did you say?
Mrs. Hill:	It's a wonderful hat, dear! Did it cost very much?
Mrs. Black:	Don't ask me, dear. I didn't have enough money. But my friend Jean had ten pounds in her purse, so it was all right.
Mrs. Hill:	I think I must have something new, too. I didn't buy a hat last year!

Step 2

A birthday present for Mrs. Hill

Unit 6

A birthday present for Mrs. Hill

Look and listen
Look, listen and repeat

Speaker:
1 The children want to choose a birthday present for their mother, | but they can't agree.

Peter:
2 I've a good idea. Let's buy a box of handkerchiefs.

Ann:
3 Not another box! She had handkerchiefs from us last year.

Mr. Hill:
4 I suggest you buy a record for your mother. | But don't choose your sort of music!

Speaker:
5 A few days later the children return home very excited.

Children:
6 No! You may not hear the record, Daddy! | It's a secret!

Children:
7 Wake up, Mummy! We have a fabulous record for you. | Listen to this latest hit!

Mr. Hill:
8 What a terrible noise! Who is howling on this record?

Children:
It's the Beethoven Boys. | Aren't they fabulous?

Questions and answers

1. What do the children want to do?
2. Who has a good idea?
3. Does Ann agree?
4. Does Mr. Hill suggest they buy a book?
5. When do the children return home?
6. May Mr. Hill hear the record?
7. What have the children got for their mother?
8. Who is playing on the record?

Drills in Drill Book 2, Unit 13

The latest hit

"Mummy," said Peter, "we want to choose a present for Daddy's birthday, but we can't agree."
"Well, now — let me think . . . . ." said Mrs. Hill.
"I've seen some lovely handkerchiefs," said Ann.
"Must you always suggest handkerchiefs?" said Peter. "We're always giving him handkerchiefs!"
"I've seen a fabulous red tie," said Tony.
"No, dear," said Mrs. Hill — "not *another* tie! Daddy had a tie from you for Christmas."
"A record?" suggested Peter.
"Now that's a very good idea!"   agreed Mrs. Hill.
"But what record?" asked Ann. "Daddy doesn't like our sort of music."
"I know!" suggested Mrs. Hill. "'The Flight of the Bumble-Bee', by Rimsky-Korsakov."
"The what?" said Tony. "Is it a hit?"
"Well, no, dear — but it's very popular, and Daddy's always wanted it."
"All right, let's buy it for him."
Two days later the children returned home very excited.
"Did you find the record?" asked their mother.
"Yes, we did," replied Tony, "and it's fabulous! There are four hits on it, and those on the other side are as good!"
"'Hits'?" said Mrs. Hill. "Did you get the right record?"
"Of course we did!" answered Peter.
"Are you sure? Let me see it."
"Oh no! You mustn't see it! It's a secret!" said Ann. "Come on Peter. Come on, Tony — let's go and hide it."

Early on Mr. Hill's birthday the children rushed into his bedroom.
"Happy birthday, Daddy!" they all shouted. "Wake up! Come and hear your birthday present!"
"Did you say 'hear' it?"
"Yes! It's a record! Mummy suggested it," said Tony.
"May we play it?" asked Peter. "You can lie in bed and listen — it's lovely and loud!"
"Yes! Let's hear it!" replied Mr. Hill.
A few seconds later a terrible noise filled the house. "Oobidoobi, oobi-doobi, doo, BAA!" it screamed.
"Isn't it fabulous?" shouted Tony. "'V-Flight', by the Bumble-Bees! It's the latest hit, and we didn't know it! Wasn't Mummy clever?"
"Doo-doo, doobi-doo!" howled the Bumble-Bees.
"Do you like your present, Daddy?" asked Ann.
"Eh? Oh! Yes. Yes! I love it. Thank you, children," replied Mr. Hill. "It's much better than handkerchiefs!"

Step 5 **1 We answer these questions**

a) What did Peter suggest as a birthday present?
b) What did Mrs. Hill reply to Peter?
c) When did the children return home excited?
d) What did Mrs. Hill ask?
e) When did the children rush into Mr. Hill's room?
f) What did they shout?
g) Did Mr. Hill really like his present?

2 Useful classroom phrases

| I'm sorry, I didn't | understand
hear | your order,
the last sentence, | Sir. |
| | bring
start
complete | the exercise,
my work,
yesterday's homework, | Madam.

Miss. |

3 Yesterday she didn't

Today is Monday, but yesterday was Sunday.
Today Mother is getting up early. And yesterday?
Yesterday **she didn't** get up early.
Today Mother is cleaning the windows. And yesterday?
Today Mother is rushing to the shops.
Today Mother is fetching some bread.
Today Mother is working in the garden.
Today Mother is telephoning the dentist.
Today Mother is talking to the postman.
Today Mother is paying for the milk.

4 We ask our neighbours questions

| Did you

Didn't you | get up late
clean your teeth
wash your face
make your bed
help your mother
eat your breakfast
come to school by bike | this morning? |

They answer with: Yes, I did *or* No, I didn't

5 Please explain what you did in the last summer holidays ●

6 These are the answers. What are the questions?

Tony's dog Bob disappeared at five o'clock. When .....?
At a quarter past five Peter visited all the neighbours. When .....?
Ann searched in the garden. Where .....?

Unit 6

Mr. Hill started the car. What . . . . . ?
Mrs. Hill discovered Bob at a quarter to nine. When . . . . . ?
The children rushed into the garage. Where . . . . . ?
Bob had three bones for his supper. How many . . . . . ?

7 What did you do a moment ago?

Pupil 1: Doreen, touch the third desk on the left. Thank you. Sit down.
          Eric, what did Doreen touch a moment ago?
Pupil 2: Doreen touched the third desk.
Pupil 1: Touch my English book, my head, my hair, my nose, my right shoe.

8 Tony can't find his pen

Tony is very angry today. He has no pen for his homework. He looks into his school bag. He searches his room. He asks his brother and calls his mother. He rushes to the supermarket, but it is already closed. After supper he discovers his pen in the dog's basket. He laughs and starts his homework.
Now tell this story again: Yesterday Tony . . . . .

9 The other man   Can you complete these sentences with the opposites?

This man   is   small   and the other is   . . . . .
This woman   thin   . . . . .

One boy   slow   . . . . .
One girl   sad   . . . . .
                     poor

10 Another pencil ●

11 Can you pronounce these words correctly?

[zd]   Daddy u**sed** Peter's bike.
[st]   Pam dan**ced** well.
[ʃt]   My sister wa**shed** my shirts.
[tʃt] We wat**ched** the athletics match.
[tid] Tony repea**ted** the teacher's sentence.
[did] The programme en**ded** at a quarter past five.

12 We copy and learn by heart

> a) *Teacher:* You must **copy** this.
>   *Peter:*   Ann **copies** it today.
>   *Ann:*   Peter **copied** it yesterday.
> b) *Teacher:* You must **say** 'please'!
>   *Peter:*   Ann always **says** 'please'.
>   *Ann:*   Peter **said** 'please' to me yesterday.
> c) *Teacher:* You must **do** your homework.
>   *Peter:*   Ann **does** her homework before breakfast.
>   *Ann:*   Peter **did** his homework yesterday afternoon.

13 Can you correct these silly sentences? ■

14 Find the odd word. A word puzzle ★

15 A game: word chains

Write a word on a piece of paper, for example: **dentist**. Then read it aloud and give the piece of paper to the pupil beside you or behind you. He must write a new word, and this must begin with the last letter of your word, a letter **'t'**. So he can write **'tooth'** or **'tea'**. Go on!

16 A competition

How many words can you make from the letters of this word: ADVENTURE?

Two examples are: 'dent' and 'read'

17 Facts about Britain

The English have a sweet tooth — in other words, they like a lot of sugar in their tea, in their cakes and puddings. An American eats 39.2 kg of sugar a year, a German 29.2 kg and a Briton 57.1 kg.

Unit 6

Unit 7

Step 1

A conversation: At the Youth Club

Ann: Where were you last night? I didn't see you in the garden.
Eileen: I went with Brian to the Youth Club.
Ann: I don't know Brian.
Eileen: Yes, you do. You saw him at our house last week.
Ann: What did you do at the club? Did you play table-tennis?
Eileen: No, we couldn't play. A silly boy sat on the ball and smashed it. So we sang songs instead and listened to the latest records. Later we drank a cup of coffee and ate chocolate biscuits.
Ann: I went to Joan's house this afternoon, and do you know who came in?
Eileen: Well, tell me, who?
Ann: Oliver Baxter! He gave me two tickets for the concert tomorrow. He can't go. Do you want to come with me?
Eileen: I'm sorry, I can't. I told Brian to fetch me. We're going to the Youth Club again.

Step 2

Eileen and Ann are in trouble

Unit 7

Look and listen
Look, listen and repeat

Eileen and Ann are in trouble

Speaker:
1 Eileen and Ann are driving in a taxi across London. | They want to catch a train at seven o'clock. | They are going to Germany.

2 There is a lot of traffic. The girls are very anxious. | Can they reach the station in time?

3 Finally they reach the station. It is five to seven. | They are in time for the boat-train to Harwich.

4 A porter takes their luggage to platform nine. | The ticket-collector wants to see their tickets.

Eileen:
5 We're in awful trouble. I can't find the tickets anywhere.
Ann:
Be quick. The train is leaving in two minutes!

Ann:
6 Perhaps the tickets are in the taxi! | Run back and get them!

Eileen:
7 But there isn't time!
Ticket-collector:
There's plenty of time! | There's another boat-train in 25 minutes, and it's for the same boat.

Porter:
8 The taxi-driver has given me these tickets.
Eileen:
Oh, thank you. Now our holiday is safe!

Questions and answers

1. Why are the girls driving in a taxi?
2. Why are the girls anxious?
3. When do the girls reach the station?
4. Where does the porter take their luggage?
5. What is this awful trouble?
6. What does Ann think?
7. When does the next boat-train leave?
8. Who has given the tickets to the porter?

Drills in Drill Book 2, Unit 14

Step 3

"There's plenty of time!"

Step 4

It was the last Friday in July, and at number two, Beech Lane, supper was just ready.
At that moment the telephone rang.
Mr. Hill answered it. "Hill here. Who's that?" he said rather angrily.
"It's Susan Bartlett. Tom — please can you help us? We're in trouble!"   5
"Oh!" replied Mr. Hill. "Hallo, Susan. What's the matter?"
"Our boat-train for our holiday in Germany leaves Liverpool Street Station in forty-five minutes, at seven o'clock. Our taxi hasn't come, and I can't find another taxi anywhere. Please, can you drive us there in your car?"
"Yes, of course!"   10
"Oh, Tom, thank you! But hurry! There isn't much time!"

Mr. Hill quickly drove the car out of the garage and met Jim and Susan Bartlett and their children, Fred und Wendy, outside their home, number fourteen, Beech Lane.
"Can you reach the station in time, Tom?" Mr. Bartlett anxiously asked.   15
"Don't worry," answered Mr. Hill. "The journey is quite short; there's plenty of time!"

But soon Mr. Hill was anxious, too: there was a lot of traffic everywhere, and again and again they had to wait at traffic-lights. They finally reached the station at one minute to seven.

"Quick, Fred!" said Mr. Bartlett. "Run and find the train, and we can all follow with the luggage. Hurry!"

Fred saw a porter — "Please, I want to find the Harwich boat-train," he said.
"Platform nine," the porter told him.
Fred ran across the station to platform nine.
There was no train there.
"Where is the boat-train?" he asked the ticket-collector.
"It went two minutes ago, sonny."
"But we must catch it! We must!"
"Sorry — you're too late for this train."
At that moment his parents, Wendy, and Mr. Hill came round the corner.
Fred sat down and burst into tears. "What can we do?" he cried.
"Catch the next train, sonny," said the ticket-collector. "There's another train in twenty-five minutes, and it's for the same boat. Didn't you know that?"
"N-no," replied Fred.
Mr. Hill laughed. "Never mind!" he said. "Your holiday is safe! Let's all go and have a cup of tea — there's plenty of time!"

Step 5

1 Let's change these sentences into questions and answer them

   a) Mrs. Bartlett telephoned at a quarter past six. (When?)
   b) Mr. Hill met the Bartletts outside their house. (Where?)
   c) "We can all follow with the luggage," said Mr. Bartlett. (What?)
   d) Fred ran across the station to platform 9. (Where?)
   e) The train went two minutes ago. (When?)
   f) "I didn't know that." (Didn't?)
   g) There is plenty of time. (Is there?)

Can you ask three more questions about the story?

2 Pam's birthday party

Pam wants **to give** a party again.
She gave a very good party last year.
She wants **to begin** the party with a game.
Last year **she began** with a song.
Peter wants **to get** an invitation.
He got an invitation last year, too.
Eric wants **to meet** Pam's friends.
Last year **he met** only Ann's friends.
Tony wants **to drink** lemonade.
Last year **he drank** seven glasses.
Ann wants **to sit** beside Denis.
Last year **she sat** beside an awful boy.
Jack wants **to bring** a nice present.
Last year **he brought** Pam a wonderful book.
Eileen wants **to come** early.
Last year **she came** at half past three.
Sheila wants **to eat** a lot of chocolate biscuits.
Last year **she ate** eleven!

3 Brian is very nosy

He asks too many questions. He always wants to know everything. He says to Ann: "I hear you went to Pam's house for tea yesterday. (to drink tea) Did you drink tea?" Ann replied:

"No, I didn't. I drank lemonade."

Go on:

Brian: (to eat cheese sandwiches)?	*Ann:* (No, tomato sandwiches)
Brian: (to sit beside Eric)?	*Ann:* (No, Denis)
Brian: (to come early)?	*Ann:* (No, to come late)
Brian: (to give Pam a new pen)?	*Ann:* (No, to give a box of handkerchiefs)
Brian: (to meet Pam's father)?	*Ann:* (No, to meet Pam's mother)
Brian: (to go upstairs)?	*Ann:* (No, to go into the garden)

Unit 7

4 It all happened yesterday

Let's write a dozen sentences about it.

I my father my sister our neighbour our grandparents your friends	found got brought back bought took home saw lost	some money a letter a wonderful present a hit record a box of handkerchiefs a tin of nuts a packet of biscuits a pound of apples a special offer an ice

Now turn your sentences into questions. Use "what" and "yesterday".

5 Ann's Sunday

Every Sunday Ann gets up at half past eight.
She brings her parents a cup of tea.
Then she has breakfast at nine.
After breakfast she goes for a walk and brings back the Sunday paper.
At half past ten she goes to church.
She eats her lunch at one o'clock.
After lunch she takes the dog for a walk.
She drinks a cup of tea at a quarter past four.
At five her friend Eileen comes, and they hurry to the park for a game of tennis.
In the evening she watches television and goes to bed at nine.

a) Yesterday was Sunday. Write down what Ann did.

b) Let's write a diary. What did you do last week?

On Monday I went to ..... On Tuesday I saw ..... On Wednesday I visited ..... On Thursday I bought ..... On Friday I met ..... On Saturday I helped ..... On Sunday I played .....

6 A holiday at the seaside

A Tony wants to go into the water and asks his father:
"May I go into the water now?"
His father replies: "Yes, you may."

Peter wants to play table-tennis and asks his mother:
"May I play table-tennis, Mummy?"
His mother replies: "No, you may not. It's too late."

a) Ann wants to buy another ice. What does she say to her mother?
b) Tony wants to eat another sandwich.
c) Peter wants to drink another glass of lemonade.
d) Ann wants to have another apple.
e) Tony wants to hear another record.
f) Peter wants to stay another minute in the water.
g) Ann wants to have another five pence for the cinema.
h) Tony wants to buy another ball.

B The holiday was last summer. Tony wanted . . . . .

7 Excuses

I couldn't come. I had to go to the dentist.

Pupil 1: Didn't you want to come yesterday?
Pupil 2: Of course I did, but I couldn't. I had to visit my grandmother.
Pupil 1: Didn't you have time yesterday?
Pupil 2: Sorry, I couldn't see you. I had to . . . . .
Pupil 1: Didn't you want to come on Monday . . . . . Tuesday, ... Wednesday . . . . .
Pupil 2: (to finish my homework, to buy a birthday present, to take my brother to the station, to help my aunt with her luggage, to go to the shops for my mother)

8 Can you pronounce these words correctly?

race, at, sad, late, match, flat, flame, ladder, hat, date, cat, fat, to wake, to hate, to crash, to waste, to take.

Now let us write two lists. In list 1 we copy all words you pronounce like 'plate' [ei]. In list two we copy all words you pronounce like 'match' [æ].

9 Can you fill the blanks? ●

10 Monica's diary ■

Unit 7

11 Uncle Bill's birthday present ★

12 A limerick

Doctor Foster went to Gloster
In a shower of rain.
He stepped in a puddle,
Right up to the middle,
And never went there again.

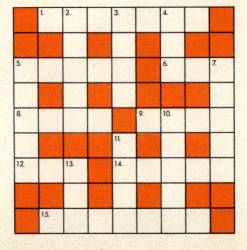

13 Facts about Britain

Big Ben is the name of the bell in the clock tower of the Palace of Westminster. Here the British Parliament meets. The House of Commons has 630 members. They are MPs = Members of Parliament.

14 A crossword puzzle

ACROSS

1. Third day of the week (7)
5. Not tomorrow but ..... (5)
6. At the ..... of the house (3)
8. They ..... two pounds (4)
9. His ..... is too long (4)
12. Peter is Mr. Hill's ..... (3)
14. Aunt Maud lives ..... (5)
15. Peter's birthday is on January.. (7)

DOWN

2. The dog's basket is ..... the table (5)
3. Our teacher always .....: Don't talk! (4)
4. Now ..... this play (3)
5. Cats often climb ..... (5)
7. I have three pounds in my ..... (5)
10. This is a book ..... England (5)
11. Peter! ..... your brother, Ann. His friends have come. (4)
13. Not an old book, but a ..... book. (3)
14. ..... children like chocolate (3)

66   Unit 7

Unit 8 — We are over London now

Meet Sabine and Carsten Grau. They are flying from Düsseldorf to London. They are very excited, of course. They have never been to England, so this is the greatest adventure of their lives. And they are not going for a short holiday. They are staying in London for a whole year. Their father is an engineer and he is going to a new job with a German firm in London. He has already bought a small flat in the London suburb of Surbiton and is waiting for them at London Airport.

British passenger: You are a German girl, aren't you? Do you understand English?
Sabine: Just a little. I have had two years of English lessons.
Passenger: Then I can explain some of the more interesting sights to you. Look, we're over the Channel now, and there are the white cliffs of Dover.
Sabine: They look lovely in the sunshine. We're very lucky. It's a wonderful day today.
Passenger: Do you see the boats down there? They are car ferries and they take cars from here to Calais in France and to Ostend in Belgium.
Stewardess: We're landing at London Airport in ten minutes. Please fill in your landing card. You must show it later to the Passport Control Officer at the airport.
Sabine: What do I write for 'occupation'?
Passenger: Just write 'schoolgirl'.
Sabine: Is that the river Thames?
Passenger: Yes, and that great church is St. Paul's Cathedral, and behind it you can see the big office blocks of the City of London.
Passenger: Now we're over the West End. And there is Piccadilly Circus.
Carsten: Where is Buckingham Palace?
Passenger: Do you see those trees there? That's Hyde Park. And that big building there is the Queen's London home. And over there is the airport.
Stewardess: Ladies and gentlemen. We are now arriving at London airport. It is Britain's biggest airport. Planes from all over the world arrive here nearly every minute of the day and night.
Sabine: We've arrived!

The pictures on page 68 show:

The white cliffs of Dover
St. Paul's Cathedral
Buckingham Palace

The River Thames
Piccadilly Circus
A Boeing 707 at London Airport

Unit 8

The harvest

1

2

3

4

5

6

Unit 8

a) Look and listen
b) Look, listen and repeat

The harvest

1 This is Jill. | She's working on her aunt's farm.

2 These two boys in the field are Jill's cousins. | They are her aunt's sons.

3 It has stopped raining. | The cousins can start with the harvest.

4 Jill has to milk the cows before seven o'clock.

5 She hates milking cows | but she doesn't want to disappoint her uncle.

6 Jill's uncle is very upset. | It has started raining again.

Step 2

A holiday on the farm

Aunt: Didn't you hear me, Jill? You must get up now! It's ten past five.
Jill: Oh dear! I'm still so tired. Do you need me this morning?
Aunt: We need everbody's help. It's stopped raining, and we must start with the harvest. Your two cousins are already working in the fields.
Jill: May I work with them?
Aunt: Later perhaps. You must milk the cows before breakfast.
Jill: Oh dear, I hate doing that. Do I have to milk them?
Aunt: You mustn't disappoint your uncle. He's waiting for you downstairs, dear. Hurry up!
Jill: Oh, all right. I don't like to disappoint him.

Aunt: After breakfast you can help me with the washing-up and then ... Oh, here is your uncle. I hope he isn't upset.
Uncle: I'm very cross!
Aunt: Don't be angry. Jill is coming down. She wants to help with the milking.
Uncle: I don't need her help. I know she hates milking the cows. Her cousins are already doing it. I'm very upset.
Aunt: Well, let Jill help in the fields. She likes helping you.
Uncle: I don't need her help today.
Jill: Please, Uncle, I wasn't able to get up earlier.
Uncle: No, you can stay in bed.
Aunt: But why? You're being silly.
Uncle: It's started raining again. The harvest must wait. I'm very upset.
Aunt: Oh, I am sorry, dear. I know! Jill and I can go into town today and do the shopping.
Jill: I love shopping!

Questions

a) Do you think that Jill heard her aunt?
   Who must get up now?
   What time is it?

b) Does Jill want to get up?
   Why doesn't she want to get up?
   Do they need Jill this morning?
   Is it still raining?
   Where are Jill's two cousins?
   What are they doing there?

c) Can Jill work with her cousins at once?
   What must Jill do before breakfast?
   What does Jill hate doing?
   Who is waiting for Jill downstairs?

d) Does Jill want to disappoint her uncle?
   What must Jill do after breakfast?
   Is Jill's uncle happy?

e) Does Jill's uncle need her help?
   Who is milking the cows?
   Why can Jill stay in bed a little longer?
   Can they start the harvest?

f) What does Jill's aunt suggest?
   Does Jill agree?

Unit 8

g) What did you do before breakfast this morning?
   Is this week the right time to start the harvest?
   Do you like milking cows?
   Do you like helping with the washing-up?
   Were you able to get up very early this morning?
   Does your mother need your help this afternoon?
   When did it start raining yesterday?
   When did it stop raining this morning?

Step 3 Drills in Drill Book 3, Unit 1

Step 4 A letter from a farm

Garden Farm,
Downham Market,
Norfolk.
4th September.

Dear Sabine and Carsten,

I am very sorry — I wanted to write to you last week, but I had to help my uncle with the harvest on his farm. Two of his men were ill, and so my uncle needed everybody's help — my aunt and my two cousins had to work in the fields, too. We had to get up at five o'clock every morning and work all day;
5 in the evenings I wasn't able to keep my eyes open, and so I went to bed at half past eight.

We got the harvest in just in time: it has not stopped raining today. But I am still very busy: this morning before breakfast I had to milk the cows (I hate doing that) and feed the hens; after breakfast I had to help my aunt with the

washing-up, and then I did the shopping for her in Downham Market. I wanted to ride into town on my uncle's horse, but I had to go by bus. — "The horse is too big and you are too young and small," my uncle told me. I was very cross! But now I have a little time before lunch, and so I am able to write to you.

Did you have a good journey to England — and do you like your new flat in Surbiton? I hope so. Why didn't you come to England a week earlier? I was very upset about that — I so much wanted to meet you at London Airport, but I had to come to my uncle's farm on August 27th. I always come here at the end of August, and my uncle and aunt look forward to my visit: I don't like to disappoint them. But I return home on the 11th, and school doesn't start until the 14th, so why don't you both come to our house for the day on the 12th? I so much want to see you again after all this time, and I am very excited about your long stay in England. A whole year! We can do a lot in the time.

My aunt is calling me for lunch. I don't want to stop writing to you, but I must go. It is hard work on a farm, but the food is lovely and my aunt is a wonderful cook. I am getting very fat!

Until next week, then. Be good! My regards to your mother and father. Do they like driving on the left-hand side of the road?

Kindest regards,
Yours,
Jill.

Unit 8

Step 5

1 Cathy asks Jill a lot of questions

Jill returned from her holiday on her uncle's farm on September 11th. The next day she met her friend Cathy. Cathy asked Jill a lot of questions. What were they? Here are Jill's answers:

Cathy:
Did you help with the harvest?

Jill:
Yes, I helped with the harvest.
No, I didn't get up late.
No, I didn't like milking cows.
Yes, I loved feeding the hens.
Yes, I was able to go shopping.
No, I couldn't ride my uncle's horse.
No, I wasn't able to watch television.
Yes, I liked staying on the farm.
Yes, I got very fat.

2 Jill's Uncle Cuthbert wants help

Jill's cousin Ronald arrives a week later. He hates helping with the harvest. So Jill's aunt Mary says to her husband Cuthbert:

Mary: Ronald hates helping.
Cuthbert: Sorry, but he just has to help.
Mary: Ronald hates getting up early.   Ronald hates fetching the horses.
Ronald hates feeding the hens.   Ronald hates riding the horses.
Ronald hates milking the cows.   Ronald hates eating in the fields.
Ronald hates drinking a lot of milk. Ronald hates working outside.

3 Please ask your neighbour what he likes or hates doing

Do you	like	eating lovely food?
		getting up at five?
Does your brother		working in the fields?
	enjoy	working all day?
Does your sister		doing the washing-up?
	love	getting very fat?
Do your parents		sitting on the floor?
	hate	eating cigarettes?
		going into town?

4 Carsten's silly cousin Oswald ●

5 Oswald prefers coffee ■

6 Jill always has to ask for permission

Aunt: I must always know where you are, Jill, and what you are doing. You mustn't worry me and your mother. What do you want to do today?
Jill: May I feed the hens before breakfast?
Aunt: **Yes, you may. But you mustn't** be late for breakfast.

Jill: May I work in the fields?
Aunt: Yes . . . forget your cousins' sandwiches.
Jill: May I go into town this afternoon?
Aunt: Yes . . . forget to take your coat.
Jill: May I do the shopping for you?
Aunt: Yes . . . lose my purse.
Jill: May I climb the old apple tree this evening?
Aunt: Yes . . . climb alone.
Jill: May I ride the horse tomorrow?
Aunt: Yes . . . ride across the fields.
Jill: May I go now?
Aunt: Yes . . . forget to close the door.

7 Carsten writes to his German friends

Carsten arrived in England on 24th August. The next day he went into town and did his mother's shopping. He could understand everybody, and everybody could understand him. He could find the supermarket and he could buy all the things on his mother's shopping list. He could find the bus stop and get the right bus home. He could see Buckingham Palace and he could stop the bus at the right bus stop.

So he sat down and wrote a letter about it to his German friends. He wrote:

Dear Uwe and Klaus,

My English isn't so bad! **I was able to go** into town and I was . . .

Please go on.

8 Sabine's English isn't so good

She doesn't understand the shop assistants.
She gets on the wrong bus.
She stops the bus at the wrong bus stop.
She doesn't understand English money.
She can't buy the things on her shopping list.
She can't understand the television programmes.
She hates going out.
She has to start learning English again.

Her mother wrote a letter about it and said:

"Sabine's English was very poor.
She **didn't understand** the shop assistants.
She . . ."

Please go on.

9 What they say in English classrooms

The pupils like to talk, but their teacher says: **Stop talking.**
The pupils like to make a noise, but . . .
The pupils like to jump up and down, but . . .
The pupils like to draw funny pictures, but . . .

Unit 8

The pupils like to shout in the music lesson, but ...
The pupils like to copy from their neighbours, but ...
The pupils like to eat chocolate in the lesson, but ...
The pupils like to speak English in the German lesson, but ...

The children hate coming early, but the teacher says:
You mustn't forget to come early.
The children hate keeping their desks tidy, but ...
The children hate learning new words by heart, but ...
The children hate closing the door, but ...
The children hate getting up, but ...
The children hate correcting their homework, but ...
The children hate washing their hands before lunch, but ...
The children hate cleaning the classroom after school, but ...

10 Sabine's English phrase-book

Sabine wanted to speak better English. So she asked Jill for advice: 'What must I do? I want to speak as well as you, Jill.' 'Learn a lot of useful new words. Learn a dozen new words a day. Increase your vocabulary, Sabine!' 'That's very good advice, Jill. Thank you.'

So Sabine started an English phrase-book. In it she wrote down a lot of useful phrases. She started with a few phrases she heard at a bus-stop:

Londoner: Excuse me, Miss, but **you must wait your turn.**
Sabine: I must wait my turn? Turn?
Londoner: Yes, you must wait until it is your turn to get on the bus. **You must stand in the queue.** Behind me!
Sabine: The queue?
Londoner: **This line of people** waiting for the bus.
Sabine: **I want to catch a bus** to Surbiton. Where is this bus going to?
Londoner: This is the right bus for you, Miss. **Hop on!**
Bus conductor: **Any more fares, please?**
Sabine: One to Surbiton, please.
Can you tell me, please, **when I must get off?**

11 The "YES-NO" game

Two pupils have to stand up. One asks the questions and the other gives the answers. But he mustn't use the words "YES" or "NO" in his answers. The pupil who answers questions with a "YES" or a "NO" gets a penalty point for his side. Here are some questions:

Are you fifteen years old?
Are you German?
Have you got a dog?
Are you happy at school?
Do you like swimming, going to the cinema, singing?
Do you have to stay at school this afternoon?
Do you want to come to school on Sunday?
Are you able to add two and two?
Have you ever been to Berlin?

12 Everything went wrong ★

Unit 9

At the greengrocer's

Step 1

1

2

3

4

5

6

Unit 9

At the greengrocer's

a) Look and listen.
b) Look, listen and repeat.

1 Jill has invited Alan to her party. | He's the most handsome boy in town.

2 Margaret is Jill's most helpful friend. She's making delicious lemonade.

3 The lemons for the lemonade | are from the most expensive greengrocer in town.

4 Brown in the High Street | is the worst greengrocer in town. | His apples are tasteless.

5 Jill must hurry to the butcher. | At the butcher's she buys the less expensive sausages.

6 At the baker's Jill meets Roger. | He's a very boring boy | and always says the most stupid things.

Step 2   **Shopping for a party**

Jill: Hallo, Margaret! Where are you going?
Margaret: I'm shopping for the party this evening. I must go to the grocer's and to the butcher's.
Jill: Who's coming to your party?
Margaret: Well, you're invited. Alan, Tom and Ronald are coming too.
Jill: The most handsome boys in town! You really give the most wonderful parties, Margaret.
Margaret: Thank you! But I must hurry. I still have a lot to do.
Jill: Can I help you with your shopping?

Margaret: Wonderful! You're my most helpful friend. Let's stop at this greengrocer's. I have to get six lemons. You make the most delicious lemonade, Jill. Can you make it for my party?

Jill: Of course. Oh, look at those lemons! This shop always has the most beautiful lemons in town.

Margaret: Yes, but look at the price. This greengrocer is also the most expensive in town.

Jill: I know this shop is more expensive than Brown's in the High Street. But Brown's has the most awful apples and lemons. The more expensive things are often cheaper in the end.

Margaret: I agree.
Oh, look, there's Roger Harper.

Roger: Hallo, Margaret. Are you having a party this evening?

Margaret: Party? Me? What gave you that idea? I'm shopping for my mother. See you later. Bye-bye!

Jill: Why did you lie, Margaret?

Margaret: I've never met a more boring boy. He never stops talking, and he says the most stupid things. I don't want to have him at my party. Ah, there's a baker's shop.

Jill: I like going to that baker. He has the most delicious cakes in town. Oh, I'm looking forward to your party, Margaret.

Margaret: Good. Come on! I must telephone Eileen. She has the latest and most exciting hit-records.

Questions

a) When is Margaret's party?
   Where is Margaret going?

b) Who are the most handsome boys in town?
   Who gives the most wonderful parties?

c) What does Margaret want to do now?
   Why is Jill a most helpful friend?

d) Who makes the most delicious lemonade?
   Does a butcher sell the lemons?
   Is this greengrocer the cheapest in town?
   Which shop is less expensive?
   What is cheaper in the end?

e) Does Margaret lie to Jill?
   Who says the most stupid things?
   Does Margaret want Roger at her party?

f) Why does Jill like going to that baker?
   What is Jill looking forward to?
   Who has the most exciting hit records?

g) What can you buy at the butcher's?
What can you buy at the grocer's?
Where can you buy lemons?
Where can you buy buns?

Which is more expensive, a pound of meat or a pound of apples?
Which is more tasteless, a glass of lemonade or a glass of water?
Which baker in your town has the most delicious cakes?
Which pupil in your class has the most beautiful English accent?
Which shop sells the most expensive dresses in your town?
Who has the most exciting hit records in your class?

Step 3 **Drills in Drill Book 3, Unit 2**

Step 4 **The party**

Jill: Sabine! Carsten! Come and meet Jennifer: she's Julia's elder sister. Jennifer — talk to Sabine and Carsten for five minutes, please: I have to go to the butcher's and the greengrocer's.
Jennifer: Of course. Hallo — are you Jill's German friends?
5 *Sabine:* Yes — we came to England a month ago. Our father is working here for a year and we're living in a new flat in Surbiton.
Jennifer: Mm — Julia told me. Why didn't you come to Margaret's party last Saturday?
Sabine: Margaret? We don't know her. Who is she?
10 *Jennifer:* Oh, she's Julia's friend. She's the ugliest girl in London, and her party was awful. I've never eaten more tasteless and less attractive

food, nor listened to more boring records. The room was very hot, and it must have been the smallest in England, full of the most uncomfortable furniture and the most stupid boys in the world: they couldn't dance and they talked nonsense. And Margaret must be the worst hostess: the coffee was cold, she ate too much, she laughed too loudly, and she never stopped talking. I went home at nine o'clock: I was so bored. Julia stayed until midnight: she enjoys parties, even awful parties — and Margaret's party was certainly awful.

Carsten: It sounds terrible. We want to have a party at our flat soon. You must come, and perhaps we can give you a much more interesting evening.
Jennifer: Ooo — thank you! May I come? You are kind!
Sabine: Yes, of course. Oh look — there's Julia!
Jennifer: Yes — well, I must go: I have to go to the library. Bye-bye!

Sabine: Hallo, Julia. Jennifer's just told us about that awful party last Saturday at Margaret's house.
Julia: Awful? It wasn't awful! It was wonderful — I've never been to a more beautiful party!
Carsten: But Jennifer said . . .
Julia: Don't listen to her! It was a lovely party — the most comfortable chairs, the most delicious and expensive food, the most exciting party-games, and the most handsome boys in town! And Margaret has all the latest hit-records: I've never enjoyed dancing so much!
Carsten: Are you talking about the same party? The boys were stupid and couldn't dance; the food was terrible; the party was boring. Jennifer told us.
Julia: Jennifer said that? Let me tell you about Jennifer: she hates going to parties, she can't dance, and she doesn't like playing party-games. At Margaret's party she sat on a settee in a corner and ate and ate and ate; she didn't dance and she didn't talk — and so nobody

	wanted to dance with her or talk to her. She ate too much and then felt ill, and so we had to send her home early. Margaret's parents drove Jennifer home in their car, and so I was able to stay at the party, and I had a most wonderful time. I have never been to a more enjoyable party. Jennifer was sick all night and had to stay in bed all Sunday — the silly girl! Look — here comes Jill. I must go. Bye-bye — see you again. And don't ever invite Jennifer to a party!
Sabine:	Bye-bye. Hallo, Jill. Jill — did you go to Margaret's party? Tell us about it. Was it nice?

Who can give the most intelligent answers?

a) Who is the younger sister?
b) When did Sabine come to England?
c) How long is Carsten's stay in England?
d) What was wrong with Margaret's food?
e) What did Jennifer say about the boys at the party?
f) Did Jennifer find her hostess attractive?
g) Why did Jennifer go home so early?
h) Why did Julia stay until midnight?
i) Where does Jennifer have to go?
j) What does Julia say about the food at Margaret's party?
k) How much did Julia enjoy the party?
l) Why was Jennifer sick all night?
m) What does Julia suggest to Sabine?

Step 5 **1 Wonderful Gordon and his family**

Sheila:	That Gordon is wonderful! He is very intelligent. Do you know his brother?
Cathy:	Oh, the brother is even more intelligent than Gordon.
Sheila:	Gordon's mother is very beautiful. Do you know his wife?
Cathy:	Oh, the wife is ...
Sheila:	His sister is fabulous. Do you know his friend?
Cathy:	
Sheila:	His aunt is very helpful. Do you know his uncle?
Cathy:	

Sheila: His cousin Dick is very interesting. Do you know his cousin Henry?
Cathy:
Sheila: His dog is very frightened. Have you seen his cat?
Cathy:
Sheila: His car is very expensive. Have you ever seen his house?
Cathy:
Sheila: His little daughter is wonderful. Have you ever seen his son?
Cathy:
Sheila: His chairs are very comfortable. Have you ever seen his settee?
Cathy:
Sheila: The apples in his garden are delicious. Have you ever eaten his cakes?
Cathy:

2 The worst food I have ever eaten

Jennifer has two friends, Muriel and Linda. They, too, hated Margaret's party.

Jennifer: The food was very bad.
Muriel: It was worse than Angela's food.
Linda: It was the worst food I have ever had.

Jennifer: The coffee was very bad.
The chocolate cake was very bad.
The ice cream was very bad.
The jam was very bad.
The meat was very bad.
The sausages were very bad.
The walnut cake was very bad.
The music was very bad.

3 Alan is very rich ●

4 Please look at the story again and correct these sentences:

a) Sabine came to England three years ago.
b) The room must have been the biggest in Germany.
c) The boys were able to dance.
d) Margaret must be the most helpful hostess.
e) Margaret laughed attractively.
f) Julia stayed until half past ten.
g) Julia never hated dancing so much.
h) Jennifer enjoyed playing party games.

5 You can choose ■

6 Which problem is the most difficult?

Problem 1: Add three and nine.
Problem 2: 69 plus 962
Problem 3: 2645×8976

a) Is problem 2 more difficult than problem 3?
b) Is problem 2 easier than problem 1?

c) Is problem 1 more difficult than problem 3?
d) Which is the most difficult problem?
e) Which is the easiest problem?

Find three more problems and ask your neighbours the same questions.

7 Ask your neighbour:

a) Who has the blackest hair in our class?
   the dirtiest shoes?
   the biggest bag?
   the whitest shirt/blouse?
   the tidiest desk?
   the nicest bike?
   the best school report?

b) What did you do before breakfast? And after breakfast?
   before the first lesson? And after the first lesson?
   before lunch? And after lunch?
   before tea? And after tea?
   before supper? And after supper?

8 At the party

This cake is delicious.
That cake is **more** delicious.
But those cakes are **the most** delicious **of all**.

a) This record is fabulous.
b) This girl is interesting.
c) This boy is stupid.
d) This chair is comfortable.
e) This game is exciting.
f) This apple is delicious.
g) This present is expensive.
h) This guest is excited.

9 It is nice to be intelligent

But a cow is **not as intelligent as** a dog.

a) horse   — man   — clever
b) cat   — girl   — big
c) fish   — elephant   — hungry
d) cow   — hen   — small
e) pupil   — teacher   — strong
f) grandson — grandfather — wise
g) my cousin — my aunt   — rich
h) boy   — teacher   — tall

10 Can you complete these rhymes?

As hot as tea
As blue as the ...
As comfortable as a chair
As long as Tom's ...

As helpful as Pat
As intelligent as a ...
As big as a farm
As long as my ...

11 This is difficult for a German

Example: It is more difficult to drive on the left.
Driving on the left is more difficult.

a) It is more difficult to ride an English bike.
b) It is more difficult to speak English.
c) It is more difficult to read an English paper.
d) It is more difficult to draw English children.
e) It is more difficult to sing English songs.
f) It is more difficult to write stories in English.
g) It is more difficult to understand English people.
h) It is more difficult to pay with English money.

12 Now the sentences are getting more and more difficult ★

13 Sabine's English phrase-book

> Yesterday I heard a few useful phrases with the verb 'may'.
>
> a) May I come in? (Can I?)
> May I have a second cup of tea?
> May I help you with that suitcase?
>
> b) You may be too late for that bus. (You are perhaps)
> You may like that new film at the City Cinema. (Perhaps you will like)
> There may be more rain this afternoon. (Perhaps there will be)
>
> c) May you be happy in England! (I hope you will be)
> May you be lucky!
> May you have a long and happy life!

14 Carsten's English scrapbook

Carsten has started to make an English scrapbook.
Perhaps you want to make a scrapbook, too?
Carsten likes drawing cars and planes. So he has drawn or cut out all the latest British cars and planes. He has stuck them in his scrapbook. Now he must label them.

15 A team game: At the greengrocer's

Please look at this sentence-table. Then divide your class into two teams, the tomato team and the orange team. The first pupil of the tomato team must make one sentence from the sentence-table. He has five seconds to do it. If he doesn't, his team gets a penalty point. If he uses the wrong pronunciation, his team also gets a penalty point. Then the first pupil of the orange team must make a sentence. A pupil mustn't choose a sentence which has already been chosen before, or he gets a penalty point.

These are Those are	the most the least	expensive delicious wonderful beautiful awful fabulous	apples lemons oranges cherries tomatoes potatoes nuts	in London. in town. in the shop. in the district.

Unit 10

Burglars!

Step 1

1

2

3

4

5

6

Unit 10

89

Unit 10

Burglars

a) Look and listen
b) Look, listen and repeat

1 Last night something awful happened. Dangerous burglars went to my aunt's house.

2 The burglars took everything. | Even the washing-machine!

3 They found the silver

4 and ran with it to their lorry.

5 They threw my aunt's clothes on the lorry.

6 They took a record-player and a typewriter.

| Step 2 | Remember, remember, the fifth of November! | |

Mrs. Sherwood: That was the last firework. Let's go back into the house, children. It's going to rain in a minute.
Mabel: I don't care. I'm staying in the garden.
Mr. Sherwood: Enough is enough. Come into the house now! Oh dear! Come and look!
Mrs. Sherwood: Oh no! Mabel, Jean, come here.
Jean: What's happened?
Mr. Sherwood: We've had burglars in the house. The whole living-room is empty.

Mrs. Sherwood: I think I'm going to cry. They've taken the television, all our records, even the washing-machine.
Mabel: They've taken my record-player, too!
Jean: And the silver from the dining-room!
Mrs. Sherwood: This is the worst day of my life.
Mr. Sherwood: My typewriter has disappeared, my clothes, everything!
Mabel: Where's the dog?
Jean: He's hiding under your bed.
Mrs. Sherwood: Oh, this is really awful. What are we going to do?
Mabel: I'm going to tell the neighbours. These burglars are dangerous.
Jean: I'm going to run to the corner. Perhaps I can still catch the burglars.
Mrs. Sherwood: I'm going to cry. How could it happen? Why didn't we hear the burglars?
Mr. Sherwood: You forget the fireworks, dear. Now, come and sit down.
Mrs. Sherwood: Where?
Mr. Sherwood: In the kitchen. They didn't take the kitchen chairs: they weren't good enough for them.
Mabel: And I'm going to make a nice cup of tea.

Please to remember — the fifth of November — gunpowder, treason and plot. Remember, remember, — the fifth of November — must never be forgot!

Questions

a) Have the Sherwoods got another firework?
   What does Mrs. Sherwood want to do?
   When is it going to rain?
   Does Mabel want to come inside?

b) Who has been in the house?
   What did the burglars forget to take?
   What is Mrs. Sherwood going to do?
   Can they watch television now?
   Whose record-player did they take?

c) Where did Mrs. Sherwood have the silver?
   What has Mr. Sherwood lost?

d) What is the dog doing under the bed?
   Why is he under the bed? Who frightened him:
   What is Mabel going to do?

e) What is Jean going to do?
Does she want to catch a policeman?
Why didn't Mrs. Sherwood hear the burglars?

f) What does Mr. Sherwood suggest?
Why didn't the burglars take the kitchen chairs?
What is Mabel going to do?

g) When do you have fireworks in Germany?
What are you going to do next lesson?
What are you going to do tonight?
Have you ever had burglars in the house?
What was the worst day of your life?

h) Your house is on fire. What are you going to do?
A burglar is climbing through your bedroom window. What are you going to do?
It has started to rain What are you going to do?
One of your aunts gives you six of the latest hit records. What are you going to do?

i) Your mother is ill in bed. What are you going to do?
Your cat has climbed a tree and can't come down. What are you going to do?
You have bought three tins of meat at the supermarket and you find that you have lost your purse. What are you going to do?

j) You have drawn a funny picture of your English teacher and he has just seen it. What are you going to do?
You are at the seaside. You have just fallen into the water, but you can't swim. What are you going to do?

Step 3 **Drills in Drill Book 3, Unit 3**

Step 4 **A November 5th**

In 1605 some men wanted to kill James I, King of England, and his whole Parliament. They dug a tunnel into the cellars under the Houses of Parliament in London, and they took barrels of gunpowder down this tunnel and into the cellars. One of the men, Guy Fawkes, stayed in the cellars. The king had to come
5 to the Houses of Parliament on November 5th, and Guy Fawkes was going to light the barrels of gunpowder on that day and destroy the Houses of Parliament and everybody in them. But someone told the king: soldiers searched the Houses of Parliament, and in the cellars they found Guy Fawkes and the gunpowder. The king was safe.

People in England still remember the Gunpowder Plot today. Children make a 'guy', dress it in old clothes, and put it in an old pram or on a box in the street. Then they ask people for 'a penny for the guy'. With this money the children buy fireworks. They build a big bonfire, put the 'guy' on the top, and, in the evening of November 5th, Guy Fawkes' Day, they light it. They cook sausages and potatoes in the fire, and let off their fireworks. Everybody has a very noisy and happy time.

B Lucky Jack

On November 5th Sabine and Carsten and some English friends went to a Bonfire Night party. On their way home they were all very happy and excited. Then one of the boys, Jack Selwood, found some fireworks in his pocket.
"I'm going to let them off!" he shouted.
"Jack, you mustn't!" said Alan, his brother. "You mustn't let fireworks off in the street! It's very dangerous!"
"I don't care: I'm not going to keep them for a whole year! Look! I've got four 'Jumping Crackers' and an 'Atomic Cannon'. That's fabulous! It makes a lovely loud noise!"

"Jack — you mustn't!"

"Come on, then — stop me!" shouted Jack, and he lit two of the 'Jumping Crackers' and threw them on the ground. Everybody ran.

"You can come home alone!" Alan shouted. "We're not going to stay with you!"

5 Jack laughed. "I don't care!" he shouted, and he pointed the 'Atomic Cannon' at his friends, and lit it.

At that moment a lorry came down the road.

'Boom!!' went the firework, and it shot across the road and hit the lorry. The driver jumped, and the lorry skidded into a wall.

10 Jack ran — and ran — and ran, all the way home . . .

Outside his house there was a police-car.

He walked slowly into the house. There were policemen in the hall, and the living-room looked different.

"What's happened?" he said.

15 "We've had burglars," said his mother. "They took almost everything — the record-player, the television, all our records, the washing-machine, the silver, your father's typewriter, your and Alan's bikes — everything."

"Oh," said Jack, and he sat down. He felt sick. He wanted to cry. Then the telephone rang.

20 His father answered it. "It's for you, Inspector," he said to one of the policemen.

"This is it," thought Jack. "They've discovered the lorry."

"Mr. Selwood," called the Inspector, "that was the police-station; we've got your things. They were on a lorry, and the lorry crashed into a wall. Some child threw a firework and the lorry skidded. The child disappeared, but we've got

25 the burglars and all your things. That child's lucky! He did a good job for us — by accident! My goodness, he's lucky!"

"Please — may I go to bed?" whispered Jack. "I'm not feeling very well."

Step 5

1 Learn by heart, please:

This morning	But yesterday afternoon
He **finds** a penny.	He **found** five pennies.
He **tells** his father.	He **told** his mother.
He **runs** to school.	He **ran** to the party.
He **buys** some apples.	He **bought** some potatoes.
He **makes** his bed.	He **made** a guy.
He **puts** a shirt into the washing-machine.	He **put** a guy on the fire.
He **lets** off a firework.	He **let** off a firework.
He **lights** a cigarette.	He **lit** a firework.
He **builds** a house.	He **built** a bonfire.
He **throws** a ball.	He **threw** a firework.

Now we write a story with the verbs on page 93

a) Jill meets Sabine and invites her to a Bonfire Party. She tells Sabine what they are going to do: "We are going to make a guy and ..."

> Look at paragraph 2 of text A and go on.

b) Two days after the Bonfire Party, Sabine met Julia and told her about the party: "We made a guy. We let off ..."

> Please go on.

2 Joan hasn't started yet

Jill: Have you made your guy?
Joan: No, I haven't made it yet.
Jill: Have you found an old pram for your guy?

> Have you bought the potatoes?
> Have you let off a firework?
> Have you built a bonfire?
> Have you thrown a firework?
> Have you told your friends about your party?
> Have you made a cake for your party?

3 Planning an enjoyable weekend

I	am		buy some new clothes	
			invite interesting friends	
My brother	is		go to the library	
My cousin		going to	eat delicious cakes	on Saturday
			stay in bed all day	on Sunday
We			dress in our best clothes	
My parents	are		dig in the garden	
My friends			ride into town	

First write twelve sentences.

Unit 10

Then ask the pupil beside you:

What are you going to do next weekend?
When are you going to get up?
What are you going to buy?
What are you going to eat?
Where are you going to go?

4 Some tenses ★

5 What is Jim planning for the half-term holiday? ■

6 I'm not going to do it! ●

7 Can you find the opposites?

I am going to sell this coat.　　　　　　　I am going to buy this coat.

a) I'm going to remember this word.
b) I'm going to leave this shop.
c) I'm going to find a purse.
d) I'm going to ask a question.
e) I'm going to get up.
f) I'm going to laugh.
g) I'm going to stop this car.
h) I'm going to sell these pictures.

8 Making plans

Your English pen-friend is going to visit you in Germany this summer. Write him or her a letter and say what you are going to do together. Here are some ideas: to look forward to; to get up at; to have breakfast; to show him or her the school; to listen to the first lesson; to have milk in the break; to go home for lunch at . . . o'clock; to go swimming; to go shopping; to meet friends; to play table-tennis; to take the dog for a walk; to watch television; to wash.

9 Margaret doesn't like Jill

Jill says:　　　　　I've just bought a new dress!
So Margaret replies: I'm going to buy a new dress this afternoon.
Jill says:　　　　　I've just bought a fabulous record. *Margaret:* . . .

　　　　　　　　　I've just met my friend.
　　　　　　　　　I've just eaten a pound of chocolates.
　　　　　　　　　I've just found a fabulous new shop.
　　　　　　　　　I've just learned a new song.
　　　　　　　　　I've just seen a wonderful new film.
　　　　　　　　　I've just invited my cousins to a party.
　　　　　　　　　I've just written a letter to my pen-friend.

10 Quite the opposite

Ken is the most stupid boy in our class,
but Robert is the most intelligent boy.

Sheila is the most awful girl in our class,
but Doreen ... (wonderful)

German is the easiest subject,
but Maths ... (difficult)

My chair is the most uncomfortable in our class,
but the teacher's ... (comfortable)

Ted uses the cheapest pencils,
but Claud ... (expensive)

Barbara's party was the most boring party,
but Sheila's party ... (exciting)

Barbara's cakes were the most delicious cakes,
but Sheila's cakes ... (awful)

11 Bad luck!

Jill wants to visit her cousin Ken. He lives in a large block of flats. Jill finds the house quite easily, but she can't find the right flat. She rings the bell at the first door on the ground floor and says: "Excuse me, does Ken Blake live here?" The woman replies: "I'm very sorry, but he doesn't." So Jill tries the flat on the first floor, but the man there has no time and doesn't know. On the third floor Jill meets a little boy. He sends her to the second flat on the fifth floor. Finally Jill reaches the fifth floor. Jill rings the bell, shouts and knocks but she gets no answer. Sadly she climbs to the seventh floor. There she sees a man and he tells her: "Ken? Yes, of course I know him. Go down to the cellar. He is cleaning his bike there."

Now tell this story again in the past. Begin with "Yesterday" and choose the right verbs: saw, shouted, tried, went down, told, rang, found, said, replied, didn't, had, sent, reached, wanted, couldn't, met, knocked, got, climbed. Don't put the words in inverted commas (" ") in the past tense.

12 This is most important

	Today	Yesterday	Just
to take	He takes it.	He took it.	He has taken it.
to dig	He digs a tunnel.	He dug a tunnel.	He has dug it.
to shoot	He shoots across the road.	He shot across it.	He has shot across it.
to hit	The lorry hits the tree.	The lorry hit it.	The lorry has hit it.
to get	He gets a present.	He got a present.	He has got it.
to feel	He feels sick.	He felt sick.	He has felt sick.
to ring	The bell rings.	The bell rang.	It has rung.
to think	He thinks carefully.	He thought carefully.	He has thought carefully.

13 Tenses ★

14 A limerick

There was a young man of Dundee
Who made three big fireworks for me;
But he dropped his cigar
In the gunpowder jar —
There WAS a young man of Dundee.

15 Carsten's English scrapbook

Carsten decided to find out who in this world speaks English. He then made a list of the countries where English is everybody's mother tongue. Here are three examples: Ireland, New Zealand, Canada. Please find other countries and draw and colour the flags of these countries.

16 Sabine's English phrase-book

On November 6th, Sabine wrote down all the words she could find to do with **furniture:**

Sabine: Have the burglars taken your furniture, too?
Mrs. Selwood: Yes, they have taken the **bookcase** from my husband's study, the big **chest of drawers** from Jack's bedroom, and the **wardrobe** from my bed-room, the **mirror** from the hall, the **sideboard** from the dining-room, the **vacuum-cleaner** from the **cupboard** in the hall, and the **curtains** from the living-room. It's awful.
Sabine: I am very sorry, Mrs. Selwood. **It's a great shame!**

17 A spelling game: Rockets and Jet Planes

Form two teams — the Rockets and the Jet Planes. The teacher is the referee and gives the signal to start: Ready, Steady, Go! Then the first member of each team spells a word and the pupil behind him (or her) must form a new word beginning with the last letter of his word. For example: The first Rocket member spells NONSENS**E**. Then the second member must find a word beginning with an E, for example EAS**Y**. Then the third member must spell a word beginning with a Y = YOUN**G**. The fourth member is too slow. He can't find a word beginning with a G in ten seconds. So the Rocket Team gets one penalty point = 5 seconds. Which team can finish in the shortest time?

18 English customs

An old London custom is the Lord Mayor's Show. Every year in November, people in the City of London choose a new Lord Mayor, and he then drives in a fine golden coach from his home, the Mansion House, through the city. Behind him follow lots of coaches — it's a real procession, almost like a German carnival procession. Something gay in grey, foggy November.

Unit 11

The paper-round

Step 1

1

2

3

4

5

6

Unit 11

The paper-round

a) Look and listen
b) Look, listen and repeat

1 Alan wants a bit of extra pocket-money. | So he's looking at the advertisements in the paper. | Perhaps he can find a job.

2 Alan is lucky | and finds work as a paper-boy. | He has to deliver papers and magazines.

3 He has to be at the paper-shop by seven o'clock.

4 Sometimes it pours with rain, | and Alan returns home with a cold.

5 But the man at the paper shop | pays Alan 25 pence an hour. | That's marvellous!

6 Alan will be able to buy a new bike soon | and save money for a new record-player.

Step 2

One pound fifty pence a week

Carsten: Will you meet me at the bus-stop on Monday morning?
Alan: Sorry, I can't. I'm starting work as a paper-boy.
Carsten: Paper-boy? What does that mean?
Alan: I'll have to be at the paper shop by seven o'clock. Then I'll deliver papers and magazines to houses in our district. It's called a paper-round.
Carsten: Oh, I see. When will you get up?
Alan: I'll have to get up at half past six.

Carsten: That's not so good. Will your parents get up at the same time?
Alan: Oh no. They'll be fast asleep.
Carsten: Will you have your breakfast before your paper-round?
Alan: No, there won't be time. But I'll be able to finish my work by eight o'clock. Then I'll have breakfast with my parents at a quarter past eight.
Carsten: I don't think it'll be a very nice job. Probably it'll pour with rain.
Alan: I don't care. I have got a raincoat, you know.
Carsten: I hate getting up early. Will it be worth it?
Brian: Of course it will. They'll pay 25 pence an hour. That's £1 50 pence a week.
Alan: And just think! I'll be able to buy a new bike soon.
Carsten: Yes, I can see it now. No more bus-fares. You'll be able to save a lot of money. It'll be worth it. I need more money than you. I want a new record-player.
Alan: Well, the answer is easy. Look at the advertisements in the evening paper. Perhaps you'll be able to find a job as a paper-boy, too.
Carsten: That's a marvellous idea! I think I'll buy a paper this evening and find a job, too.

Questions

a) Where and when does Carsten want to meet Alan?
   What work is Alan going to do?

b) What will Alan have to do as a paper-boy?
   When will Alan have to get up?

c) Will Alan's parents get up at the same time?
   Will Alan have breakfast before his paper-round?

d) When will he be able to finish his paper-round?
   What will Alan do after his paper-round?

e) Does Carsten like Alan's new job?
   Why doesn't Alan care about the rain?

f) Does Carsten like starting work before seven?
   What will the stationer pay Alan for his round?

g) What will Alan buy very soon?
   Why will it be worth it?
   Where can you find advertisements for paper-boys?
   What is Carsten going to do?

Unit 11

h) When will you get up tomorrow morning?
At what time will you have breakfast?
Will your parents have breakfast at the same time?
Will you be able to finish breakfast by a quarter past seven?
Will you be able to save money next month?
Will you need more than three marks a week?
Will you have to do homework on Sunday?
Will you have to clean your teeth before supper tonight?
Will you be able to buy your mother a nice birthday present?
Will you be able to get a job in the next summer holidays?
Will you be able to finish your homework by two o'clock?
Will you be able to buy a new record-player by July 1st?

Step 3   Drills in Drill Book 3, Unit 4

Step 4   **The paper-boy**

"Dad, can I have one pound twenty-five?"
"One pound twenty-five! What for?"
"Frank, Norman, and Carsten are going to a jazz concert on Saturday week at the Royal Festival Hall, and I want to go with them. Add the train and bus
5   fares, and it will cost one pound twenty-five pence."
"No, Tom, I'm sorry: it's too much. You can't have one pound twenty-five pence for a jazz concert."
"Oh, please, Dad!"
"No. It's too expensive. You'll have to miss it, or you'll have to earn the money."
10   "But how can I earn one pound twenty-five in ten days?"
"I don't know how. Why haven't you saved your pocket-money? Do a news-paper-round: go to the stationer's at this end of the High Street — you know, Mr. Jones's shop. He'll probably have a job for you: he always needs help. Ask him."

"Mr. Jones, can I help you to deliver newspapers next week?"
"Why, Tom! How lucky! Yes, you can. I was just going to put an advertisement in the window for a paper-boy. One of my boys will be on holiday next week and I shall need extra help for six days."
"Oh, good! How much shall I earn?"
"I'll pay you twenty-five pence an hour."
"Marvellous! How long shall I have to work?"
"From seven until eight, Monday to Saturday. You'll have to be at the shop by seven o'clock in the morning, and you'll have to deliver papers and magazines to three roads. Will you be able to do that? You'll have to make up your mind quickly — I'll be able to find another boy for the job easily."
"Well — I don't usually get up before a quarter to eight, but I want the money very much. Yes, I'll do it. Thank you, Mr. Jones."
"All right. I'll see you on Monday. Remember — seven o'clock, and don't be late!"

And so Tom became a paper-boy for a week. He did not like getting up at half-past six in the morning, but he very much wanted to go to the jazz concert with his friends — and he liked the thought of the extra twenty-five pence.
Monday and Tuesday were all right: the weather was good and he found the paper-round quite interesting. But on Wednesday it was cold, and a large, fierce dog attacked him. Tom returned home very late that morning and had to miss his breakfast or be late for school. By Thursday Tom was very tired, and it poured with rain. On Friday it rained again, and Tom was even more tired, and very fed up. Then an old lady ran after him down the road and angrily asked for her weekly magazine, and Tom had to run back to Mr. Jones's shop for it. He missed his breakfast, and he was late for school, and so he had to stay behind at the end of the day. On Saturday he had a cold — but he also had his one pound fifty: one pound twenty-five for the concert, and twenty-five pence extra. It was worth it!

Tom and his friends arrived at the Royal Festival Hall ten minutes before the start of the jazz concert. It was warm and comfortable in there, and Tom felt very content and happy. The concert was marvellous — but Tom didn't hear it. The extra twenty-five pence was in his hand, there was a smile on his face — and he was fast asleep!

Will you be able to answer these questions?

a) How much money did Tom want from his father?
b) Why did he want the money?
c) Did his father give him the money?
d) Who always needed help?
e) How much did Mr. Jones offer Tom?
f) When did Tom start work?
g) How many roads were there in the paper-round?
h) How long did he need for the paper-round?
i) What did the large, fierce dog do?
j) What did he have to do at the end of the day?
k) Did Tom miss his supper?
l) How did Tom feel at the concert?

Step 5   1   **Jim is going to cycle to Germany.** He explains his plans to his friends:

I'm going to pack all my things.
Then my suitcase **will be full.**

I'm going to earn a lot of money for the journey. Then I shall be . . .
My mother is going to wash all my shirts. Then they . . .
I'm going to find a good bed for the night. Then I . . .
I'm going to buy a lot of presents for my friends. Then they . . .
I'm going to cycle ten hours every day. Then I . . .

2 Sabine talks to Jill

"I'll give you a wonderful party next week. I hope you'll come. Peter and Tony are very kind: they'll bring their fabulous records. We'll dance, and I'll invite my new friends. They'll like you, and you'll find them very handsome. You'll have to stay until midnight. It'll be an exciting party. Say you'll come, or I'll never speak to you again."

Now please write this conversation as a letter and use the long forms. Begin:

    Dear Jill,
          I shall give you . . .

3 Ask your neighbours

Are you going to	buy an evening paper	tonight?
	get a new hit record	this afternoon?
	have cocoa or milk	at break?
Are we going to	listen to the radio or watch television	this evening?
	go home by bus or walk	this morning?
Will you	be at the concert	tonight?
Will your sister	be at home	tomorrow night?
Will our teacher	forget to test us	next week?
Will we	feel tired	by midnight?
Will your parents	be content	when they see your report?
Will I	feel sad	when I leave school?

And now your neighbours can answer:

I'm going to	buy a magazine	next Saturday.
I'm not going to	get a hit record	this afternoon.
We're going to	have lemonade	at break.
We're not going to	watch television	this week.
I shall	be at the concert	by eight o'clock.
My sister will	be at home	by half past eight.
Our teacher will	remember to test us	by next Tuesday.
We shall	feel very well	by midnight.
My parents will	be most unhappy	when they see my awful report.
You will	feel wonderful	when you leave school.

4 Plans for tonight ●

5 Silly Sally never knows what to do

What	shall I shall we will you will your parents will they	do	this evening? tomorrow? the day after tomorrow? next week? in the holidays? next autumn?

Please write down ten of Sally's silly questions and then help her with some answers. Start each answer with "Why don't you . . . ?"

For example: Why don't you walk along the River Thames?
Why don't you do a paper-round and earn some money?
Why don't you go to a jazz concert?

6 I'll see you in ten minutes. Old Mrs. Cox ■

7 How old are you?

How old were you on your last birthday, Tom?
I was twelve, John.
How old will you be on your next birthday, Tom?
I'll be thirteen, of course.

Go on and ask your neighbours.

8 Ted and Bert, the burglars

Last week, Ted and Bert found 16, Prince Philip Lane, empty. The children and their parents were at a party. So Ted said to Bert: What are we going to take?

And Bert replied: **Let's take the silver.**
And Ted said: **All right, we'll take the silver.**
Bert: Let's take the television.　　　　*Ted:* All right, . . .
　　　Let's take all their clothes.
　　　Let's take the boxes in the cellar.
　　　Let's take the expensive coat.
　　　Let's take the record-player.
　　　Let's take the washing-machine.
　　　Let's take the typewriter.
　　　Let's take the pram.
　　　Let's take the furniture.

9 We'll have to hurry!

It's really awful. The children have got up much too late again. So their mother says angrily:　　　　You must hurry!

And the children agree: **Yes, we'll have to hurry.**

Mother: You must be quick in the bathroom.
You must dress in three minutes.
You must have a quick breakfast.
You must get your coats.
You must say good-bye to your father.
You must run to the bus-stop.
You must come back early this afternoon.
You must cook the supper this evening.

10 What will you do?

a) Your house is on fire.   *Answer:* I shall ring the ...
b) A burglar is climbing into your house.   *Answer:* I ...
c) You have a very bad tooth.
d) Your father's car doesn't start.
e) An old woman is afraid to go across the street.
f) You are staying on a farm in the summer. The farmer is very busy.
g) Your mother is ill in bed.
h) You want to go to the station and catch a train, but all the buses are full.

11 Lazy Ronald ■

12 Please write this story: An expensive invitation (Look at the pictures below)

Last Wednesday _ _ _ _ _ at Maud's house. Maud opened _ and the _ _ her a letter. It was an invitation to a _ on Saturday.
Maud _ upstairs to her bedroom and _ at her _. They were all old and awful. So Maud _ to the _stop and _ into _. She went into a _shop and said to the _: "I want _ _ a new party_ please."
The clever _ also _ her a wonderful _ and a new _.
On the way home it started to _ and poor Maud got very _.
On Saturday Maud was _ _ and she _ go to the party. She was very _.

Unit 11   107

13 A letter to Elizabeth: can you translate for her? ★

14 Carsten's English scrapbook:

Carsten went to Kew Gardens yesterday. These Botanical Gardens are in London, and he saw many plants, trees and flowers there. Most of them he knew from Germany; but of course he didn't know their English names. So he drew them in his scrapbook and wrote the English names underneath.

15 An acting game:

Divide the class into two teams, the policemen and the drivers. The first policeman gives an order to the first driver: "Get out of your car!" Then the driver must mime the order and say what he (or she) is doing: "I'm getting out of my car." Then the second driver gives an order to the policeman: "Take me across the road, please!"

Please go on with these orders and others:

Please stop that car. Please start my car for me. Tell me what the time is. Show me the way to the station. Find my dog for me. Pick up that piece of paper. Follow those robbers. Telephone the fire-brigade. Catch my horse. No parking here — pay two pounds. Put on your lights. Show me your papers. Light a match for me.

16 Sabine's English phrase-book

Will you be back for lunch, dear?
No, I'll stay in town.
You'll need a coat, dear. It's going to rain.
Oh, **I won't bother. I'll manage.**
Don't be silly. **Better be safe than sorry.**

17 Who will be the first to solve this puzzle? ● ■ ★

18 How good is your English? ● ■ ★

19 Sabine's shopping-list ●

Unit 12

Miss Peabody's bad memory

Step 1

1

2

3

4

5

6

Unit 12

Miss Peabody's bad memory

a) Look and listen
b) Look, listen and repeat

1 Old Miss Peabody has a very bad memory. | Today she's gone to the wrong butcher's shop.

2 The owner of this shop is Mr. Bennett. | His shop is next to the car-park.

3 Miss Peabody's butcher is really Mr. Robertson. | But his shop is next to a big filling-station | in the middle of the town.

4 Mr. Bennett looks just like Mr. Robertson. | So Miss Peabody asks him for a pound of his best meat.

5 Now Miss Peabody wants to pay her bill | but she has forgotten her handbag, as usual.

6 Miss Peabody hurries home. | But she can't open her door without a key. | It's in her handbag! And that's in her flat!

| **Step 2** | **You won't forget, will you?** | |

Old lady: Hallo, my boy. How are you? I haven't seen you since last April. You haven't forgotten me, have you?
Alan: I'm not sure.
Old lady: Of course, you haven't. I'm old Mrs. Dinsdale.
Alan: I've a very bad memory. I can't remember you.
Old lady: You're not very polite, are you? I hear your parents are buying a new house.
Alan: Certainly not.
Old lady: You'll like the new house, won't you?

Alan: No, we shan't. We'll stay in our old house.
Old lady: Tell me, you will go to Brighton again next summer, as usual, won't you?
Alan: No, we shan't. We'll go to Devon and later to Cornwall.
Old lady: But you can't leave your nice house in Brighton empty, can you? And you won't disappoint your old aunt there, will you?
Alan: I'm afraid we haven't got a house in Brighton!
Old lady: Now don't be silly. It's a yellow house in the middle of the town, one mile from the big filling-station.
Alan: We've never had a house in Brighton.
Old lady: But you're Colin Robertson-Smythe, aren't you?
Alan: Certainly not. I'm Alan Bennett.
Old lady: You're not, are you? You're just saying it for fun. You look just like dear Colin.
Alan: I really am Alan. I live in the house next to the car-park. My father is the owner of the butcher's shop on the corner.
Old lady: I can't understand it. But give my regards to your mother, won't you? You won't forget, will you?
Alan: I don't think my mother will know your name.
Old lady: Oh dear, oh dear. You really have got a bad memory. It's very sad. Good-bye, dear boy. Good-bye, Colin!

Questions

a) When did the old lady last see Alan?
   What did the old lady hear about Alan and his parents?
   Where will Alan stay?

b) Will Alan go to Brighton as usual?
   Where will Alan and his parents go next summer?
   Where is the yellow house in Brighton?

c) Has Alan's father ever had a house in Brighton?
   What is Alan's second name?
   Where is Alan's house?
   Is Alan's father the owner of a supermarket?

d) Will Alan's mother know Mrs. Dinsdale's name?
   Who has the better memory? Alan or Mrs. Dinsdale?
   What does Mrs. Dinsdale call Alan at the end?

e) Where will you go for your holiday next summer?
   Have you got a good memory?
   Have you seen your aunt since last May?
   What is your first name?

Step 3 Drills in Drill Book 3, Unit 5

Step 4 **Poor Miss Dinsdale!**

The policeman walked towards Miss Dinsdale's car. "Excuse me, madam," he said politely, "but will you show me your driving-licence, please?"

"Certainly!" said Miss Dinsdale. "It's in my handbag. Just a moment.... Oh! It's not here! It must still be in my bedroom at the hotel."

5 "The Grand Hotel, in Brighton, madam?"

"Yes! Why? Have you found it? Oh, you are clever, aren't you! Now I shan't have to return to Brighton — thank you so..."

"Madam, will you listen to me, please? We have followed you for several miles. This car was stolen from the Grand Hotel early this morning, so will you come
10 with me to the police-station, please? You'll have to answer a lot of questions, I'm afraid. And you won't be silly, will you? Thank you, madam."

* * * * *

Miss Dinsdale was a clever woman, but she had an awful memory. She always forgot something — often a lot of things.

Everything went wrong on her journey to Brighton. In the middle of the after-
15 noon the car suddenly stopped: the petrol-tank was empty. She then had to walk four miles to the nearest filling-station, and so she reached Brighton very late in the evening. Then she couldn't remember the name of her hotel, and she only found the right hotel two hours and sixteen wrong hotels later. It was then ten o'clock at night, and she had to leave early the next morning to continue her
20 journey to Cornwall. "I'm very tired," she thought: "I'll go to bed now and have a good rest." But poor Miss Dinsdale! She couldn't find the key of her suitcase — it was at home! She had to go to bed hungry, unwashed, and very tired!

The next morning Miss Dinsdale got up early — still tired after a bad night. She had a long journey in front of her, but it was a lovely day and the sun was shining. So she ordered breakfast, paid her hotel bill (she remembered to do that!), and hurried out to the hotel car-park. Her car was a blue Mini — and there it was, next to two other blue Minis! She went up to the nearest Mini, and got in.
"Madam! Madam!"
It was the hotel-porter.
"Madam! You've forgotten your suitcase! You won't go without it, will you?"
"Oh — goodness! Thank you so much," was her reply.
Miss Dinsdale drove out of the car-park, with her suitcase in the car — but, as usual, poor Miss Dinsdale's troubles were not over. On the ground in the middle of the car-park was her handbag — and next to it was a blue Mini without an owner, and a very angry young man: his blue Mini was not there!

Two hours later, Miss Dinsdale stopped at a filling-station on the road to Cornwall. She couldn't understand it, but the car needed more petrol. Suddenly a police-car drove into the filling-station, and stopped. A policeman got out. The policeman walked towards Miss Dinsdale's car. "Excuse me, madam," he said politely . . .

Step 5 **1 Questionnaire**

A very silly man came to the front-door yesterday and asked a lot of stupid questions. So I just replied "No, I shan't!" or "No, he won't!" or "No, they won't!". Please fill in the replies for me, will you?

1. Will you buy a new handbag for your girl-friend next year?
2. Will your brother buy a new hit record next month?
3. Will your parents buy a new television next year?
4. Will you save money for a new typewriter next year?
5. Will your brother need a new coat next year?
6. Will you read children's books next year?
7. Will you buy Puss-Puss cat food next year?
8. Will your parents give you more pocket-money next month?
9. Will you buy your mother a birthday present as usual?
10. Will you do your shopping in the middle of the town?
11. Will your friends buy their clothes in the shop next to the supermarket?
12. Will you please answer my questions more politely?

2 Please write a story

about Miss Dinsdale and her awful memory. You may use these words:

Last week — to go out — to want to see the film "The Burglars in the Cellar" — But, to take the wrong bus — to have to walk — to stand in front of the cinema — to be in the wrong cinema — not "The Burglars in the Cellar" but "An exciting film for the very young: Pinky and Perky go to the Moon". — Miss Dinsdale to go to a café — but no money — to lose her purse — to have to walk home four miles — to lose her way — to arrive at the front door — to have forgotten her key — to go to a hotel — to go to bed hungry, unwashed and very tired.

3 Mother is having a short holiday

Mother is going to her sister's house for a week, but, of course, she worries, and she wants to be sure. So she says to her daughter:

"Look after Daddy, please. **You'll look after Daddy, won't you?"**
Make the tea in the morning. You'll ...

Work hard.
Write every day.
Get up in time.
Pay the milkman.
Feed the dog.
Do the washing-up.
Visit your grandmother.

Don't forget to order the meat. **You won't forget to order the meat, will you?**

Don't forget to go to the greengrocer's.
Don't forget to make a pudding on Sunday.

Don't forget to do your homework.
Don't forget your father's shoes.
Don't forget to invite your uncle to tea.
Don't forget to help our neighbour.
Don't forget to take a coat to school.

4 Father doesn't like his daughter's cooking

Of course Father is not too happy about his wife's holiday.
He tells his friends about his daughter's cooking:

I ate only sandwiches.   I ate **nothing but** sandwiches!
I drank only sweet lemonade.   I drank . . .
I got only dry biscuits.
I had only cornflakes for supper.
I saw only our dog.
I heard only my daughter's school stories.

5 Miss Dinsdale hasn't got many friends

She hasn't got many friends, but she likes her cousin Mildred. Mildred always agrees.

Miss Dinsdale: The Grand Hotel is very comfortable.
Mildred: Yes, **it's** very comfortable, **isn't it**?
Miss Dinsdale: My memory is really awful.
Mildred: Yes, it's . . .
Miss Dinsdale: The hotel is very warm.
Mildred: Yes, it's . . .
Miss Dinsdale: Dinner at the hotel is very expensive.
The hotel porter is very polite.
Brighton is very attractive.
The car-park is very noisy.

Miss Dinsdale: Your brother has a marvellous car.
Mildred: Yes, **he has** a marvellous car, **hasn't he**?
Miss Dinsdale: Your brother has a very dangerous dog.
Your brother has a very ugly house.
Your brother has a very uncomfortable armchair.
Your brother has a very interesting job.

Miss Dinsdale: I drove very slowly.
Mildred: Yes, you drove very slowly, **didn't you**?
Miss Dinsdale: I packed my suitcase very badly.
I made up my mind very quickly.
I did everything wrong.
I stupidly forgot my handbag.
I couldn't find the key of my suitcase.

6 Sister Angela shops very carefully

7 Mr. Cook needs help ■

8 Miss Dinsdale's sister Angela always wants to make up her own mind.

Miss Dinsdale: *Angela:*

I will leave early.   **I won't** leave early.
I will start my journey.   . . . . .
I will have a good rest after supper.   . . . . .
I will get some petrol at the filling-station.   . . . . .
I will pay this bill at once.   . . . . .
I will take my new handbag.   . . . . .
I will park next to the blue Mini.   . . . . .
I will invite the owner of the other Mini.   . . . . .

Now ask the pupil sitting beside you: What will you do next Sunday?
Will you get up early? Will you have a big breakfast?
Will you work as usual? Will you drive to the seaside?
Will you read this book? Will you have tea at home?
Will you have a good rest in the afternoon?
Will you take the dog for a walk? Will you go to bed hungry?
Will you go to bed unwashed? Will you kiss your dog good night?

And the pupil sitting beside you will answer angrily:
No, I won't get up early!   I'll get up very late.
Please go on.

9 New Year resolutions ●

10 Carsten is alone in the house

What will he have to do?

The bell is ringing.   **He will have to** open the door.
The dog is hungry.   (to get the dog food out of the larder)
The telephone is ringing.   (to answer it quickly)
It has started to rain.   (to close all the windows)
The house is on fire.   (to telephone the fire-brigade)
A burglar is climbing through a window.   (to call the police)
The milkman is coming.   (to pay him)

11 Sabine's English phrase-book

Claud: There's a good film at the cinema. Are you going to see it?
Maud: **I'm not quite sure.**
Claud: Can you be ready by seven o'clock?
Maud: **I don't think so.**
Claud: Can you meet me outside the stationer's?
Maud: **Probably.** I don't know. **I can't make up my mind.**
Claud: You never can, can you?

12   English customs

The English eat differently. They hold their forks with the prongs downwards. So eating is rather difficult!

13   Peas

I eat my peas with honey,
I've done it all my life,
It makes the peas taste funny,
But it keeps them on the knife.

A limerick

There was a young man of Calcutta
Who spoke with a terrible stutter.
He said "If you please
Will you pass me the cheese
And also the b-b-b-bread and b-b-b-b-b-butter?"

14   Carsten's English scrapbook

Carsten went and had a look at the Surbiton Shopping-Centre yesterday. It is built round a big square. On the one side there is a tobacconist's, a chemist's, a stationer's and the Post Office. Then you can go across the Zebra Crossing to the other side. There you'll find a butcher's, a grocer's and a greengrocer's, a car park, parking meters, a bank and a self service café. Carsten drew a map of the Shopping-Centre. What about you?

15   You will remember this, won't you?

I shan't play football. I'll play tennis.
You won't play in the field. You'll play in the garden.
He won't get coffee. He'll get lemonade.

We shan't eat bread. We'll eat potatoes.
You won't go to bed at midnight. You'll go to bed at nine.
They won't go home. They'll stay behind at school.

16   A letter to Caroline: can you translate for her? ★

Unit 12

Unit 13

Westminster

Step 1

1

2
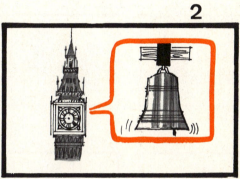

3

4

5

6

Unit 13

Westminster

a) Look and listen
b) Look, listen and repeat

1

2

1 This famous building | is the Palace of Westminster. | Parliament meets here.

2 Big Ben is the nickname for this bell. | It hangs in the tower | of the Palace of Westminster.

3

4

3 This bridge goes to the Royal Festival Hall. | This concert hall is on the opposite bank | of the River Thames.

4 Lots of famous Englishmen | lie in Westminster Abbey. | The Abbey is a big church.

5

6

5 This American tourist is in a hurry. | She wants to take a lot of photographs.

6 "Bobby" is the nickname for a London policeman. | This Bobby says: | "Parking is forbidden over there."

Step 2 Aren't your policemen wonderful!

American tourist
(lady): Excuse me, my dear, is this the St. Paul's Cathedral?
Sabine: I don't think so. I'll ask my friend. She's a Londoner.
Jill: No, this is Westminster Abbey. I thought everbody knew that. A lot of famous Englishmen lie here.
Tourist: Big Ben, too?

Jill:	No, Big Ben is the bell in the tower there, near the river. On the opposite bank of the Thames you can see the Royal Festival Hall.
Tourist:	So much English history! So many famous buildings! I must take a lot of photographs. Is that a museum there?
Jill:	Oh, no, that's Parliament, the Palace of Westminster.
Tourist:	Where the Queen lives!
Jill:	Good heavens, no! The Queen lives in Buckingham Palace.
Tourist:	Oh dear! I'm in a hurry and must get there quickly. Everybody in New York told me: You must see the Queen's home.
Sabine:	How long are you staying in London?
Tourist:	Only one day, dear. We're going for a trip to Paris, France, tomorrow, and then to Rome, Italy. Whom can I ask about the nearest way to Buckingham Palace?
Jill:	A Bobby is just coming.
Tourist:	A Bobby? Nobody speaks English here.
Jill:	A Bobby is our nickname for a policeman.
Tourist:	Oh, a policeman. Why didn't you say so? I've always heard your policemen are wonderful. So polite and so tall!
Sabine:	And they can tell you everything about London.
Tourist:	Hi there!
Policeman:	Good morning, madam. Can I help you?
Tourist:	Isn't he wonderful? Yes. Please tell me the best way to your dear Elizabeth's home.
Policeman:	Whose home?
Tourist:	The Queen's home, of course.
Policeman:	Oh, now I understand. Do you want to go by bus?
Tourist:	I want to go by car. That's my car over there.
Policeman:	Well, I'm very sorry, madam, but parking is forbidden over there. I must ask you to come with me to the nearest police station.
Tourist:	Police station? But everybody knows, London policemen...
Sabine and Jill:	Are wonderful!
Policeman:	I'm sorry. I don't think you understand.
Jill:	This lady to whom you are talking is an American tourist. She has only one day in London.
Policeman:	Oh, all right. I'll forget it. I hope you'll have a good day in London, madam.
Tourist:	You are a darling! I'll tell all my friends in New York. English policemen, er, Bobbies...
Policeman:	I know. We're wonderful!

Questions

a) Whom is the American tourist asking about St. Paul's?
Who lies in Westminster Abbey?
Is Big Ben a tower?
What can you see on the opposite bank of the Thames?

b) In which famous building is Parliament?
Where does the tourist want to go quickly?
Where is the tourist going the next day?
What is the Londoner's nickname for a policeman?

c) Who can tell you everything about London?
Whose home is Buckingham Palace?
Does the tourist want to go there by bus?
Is it forbidden to park in a car park?

d) Where does the policeman want to take the tourist?
Is the policeman going to take her to the police station?
To whom is the tourist going to say: "Bobbies are wonderful"?
What does everybody know?

e) To whom are you speaking now?
Who do you see on your left-hand side?
With whom do you go home after school?
Whose records do you like?
Whose English exercises are best?
Whose shoes are cleanest?
Who do you love most?
To whom do you give a birthday present every year?
To whom do you write a letter every Christmas?
To whom do you say good-night every evening?

* * * * *

Drills in Drill Book 3, Unit 6

Step 3

Step 4

A **London's river**

London frightens a lot of people. It is noisy, dirty, full of people and buses and cars and taxis. Everybody is in a hurry and nobody has time to stop.
But look again, and you will see another London. In this London you will find beautiful buildings, interesting museums, large parks — and London's great river, the River Thames, 'Old Father Thames' (in the words of the song). It is very dark and dirty, but it flows past a lot of London's most famous buildings. You can go on a boat-trip up (or down) London's river. Boats leave every twenty minutes, and there is usually someone to tell you the names of the famous buildings and bridges on your journey. Sabine and Carsten went on one of these boat-trips, from Westminster to Greenwich, and this is Sabine's description of the trip: —

B **Sabine's diary:** Saturday, 10th February

"Today I went for a trip with Carsten and several of our English friends down the River Thames. There was a lot of wind, but it was a wonderful trip. Here is a description of it. We started from Westminster: the Houses of Parliament were behind us and the Royal Festival Hall was on the opposite bank of the river. Each of us had a camera and we all took a lot of excellent photographs. We passed under a lot of bridges — first the beautiful, modern Waterloo Bridge, and later Tower Bridge. This bridge can divide into two sections and let big ships go through. I also saw Cleopatra's Needle and St. Paul's Cathedral, and the Tower of London.
"After Tower Bridge we passed lots of warehouses and docks and big cargo-ships. Here, in the Port of London, the sky was full of cranes and the river was full of ships and barges and tugs. In the cold light of a February day everything looked very dirty.

"Then there was a bend in the river, and suddenly we saw the tall masts of the famous sailing-ship, 'The Cutty Sark', and, behind them, the hill of Greenwich Park: our trip was almost over. Soon, much too soon, we were on a bus back to the West End.

5 "I want to go on the river again, to Hampton Court — the river there is beautiful, someone said. There are lots of swans, and there are fields on each bank. It must be lovely — but first I'll wait for the summer, the sun, and the warmer weather!"

Each of you must be ready to ask or answer a question:

a) Why does London frighten a lot of people?
b) What is the name of London's great river?
c) Can you tell us the name of a famous building in London?
d) Is Waterloo Bridge very old?
e) Did Sabine go on her boat-trip on a summer's day?
f) Where do the cargo-ships lie? Near the Houses of Parliament?
g) What can you see on each bank of the river near Hampton Court?

Step 5

1 **Class 4 B is going on a boat-trip** ●

2 **Questions about ports and ships**

After the trip down the Thames Mr. Dean asked lots of questions.

> What must every town near the sea have? (a port)
> Every town near the sea must have a port.

a) What must every port have? (docks)
b) What must every dock have? (warehouses)
c) What must every sailing-ship have? (a mast)
d) What must every cargo-ship have? (a crane)
e) What does every barge need? (a tug)
f) What does every river need? (bridges)
g) What does every sailing-ship need? (wind)
h) What does every passenger-ship need? (passengers)

3 They wanted a bun each

Jill: Did they buy a bun each?
Cynthia: Yes, **they each bought** a bun.
Jill: Did they buy a picture of London each?
Did they buy a packet of sweets each?
Did they ask for an ice-cream each?
Did they take home a book each?
Did they take a photograph each?
Did they buy an orange each?
Did they buy a lemonade each?
Did they buy a flag each?

4 Please read Sabine's Diary again ■

5 Each of you will have to remember this:

Mother is talking	Father isn't listening
Mrs. Rogers has a new handbag.	**Who** has a new handbag?
I also saw Mrs. Field today.	**Who** did you see?
Mrs. White's cat has disappeared.	**Whose** cat has disappeared?
I got a nice book from Mrs. Brown.	From **whom** did you get a book?

Can you go on and ask Father's questions?

Mother: Mr. Bloggs has a new car.   *Father:* ...?
I met Alan this morning.
I saw Doreen's uncle.
I talked to Bert's wife.
Miss Little jumped into the river.
I visited the dentist today.
I bought Sheila's washing-machine.
I went for a walk with Eileen.
I liked Dorothy's new dress.

6 Father wants to hear it once more ★

7 What, Where, When, Who, Whose, Whom?

Sabine told her father about the boat-trip down the Thames, but he didn't listen and had to ask again:
Sabine: We arrived at the river at half past nine.
Father: **When** did you arrive?
Sabine: The boat started from the opposite bank.
We all took a lot of photographs.
The barges looked very dirty.
Our teacher's description of the Tower was interesting.
We saw a lot of soldiers.
We gave a lot of bread to the swans.
Our trip was over at half past eleven.
I went home with Carsten's friend Brian.
Brian gave Carsten a book about the Tower.

8 A square in Greenwich

Please look at the picture of this square in Greenwich.
Where is everything?

a) What is **next to** the filling-station? And next to the car park?
b) Which shop is **opposite** the greengrocer's?
c) What is going **past** the greengrocer's?
d) How can you get **across** the river?
e) Is the bus stop **near to** the supermarket?
f) What can you see **in the middle** of the river?
g) Is the fire-engine going **towards** the museum?
h) Is the clock-tower **on the south side** of the square?
i) Is the Mini car stopping **in front of** the butcher's?
j) What is on the **left-hand side** of the supermarket?

9 You must make up your mind. A test ● ■ ★

10 We write a page in your diary

A boat-trip down the Rhine

You may use these words: On Sunday July 24th — to go on a boat-trip — to take a camera — to take a photograph of a friend — to start from — to go past a lot of — to see several — to leave the boat at — to have lunch at — to go for a walk — soon, much too soon, to go back.

11 Boys from different classes

1st boy: Can many of you play bridge?
2nd boy: No, very few of us can play bridge.

a) Can many of you ride a horse?
b) Can many of you milk a cow?
c) Can many of you take good photographs?
d) Can many of you play Rugby football?
e) Can many of you dance the Tango?
f) Can many of you give a description of Paris?
g) Can many of you speak American English?
h) Can many of you drive a crane?

Now change sides!

12 A grand competition! Try it!

Who can write the most sentences in the shortest time?

There are	a lot of lots of a few many several a dozen	polite boys attractive girls dirty shoes untidy desks unwashed pupils good readers bad writers	in this class. on the left. on the right. in the first row. at the back of the room. in front of me. behind you.

13 Quick! Make a sentence!

Someone Somebody Everybody Nobody	in my family in our house in our block of flats on our farm in this row	has	a very old watch. a big head. black eyes. dark hair. very big feet. a red nose. a good memory. a famous father. lots of fine photographs. several good records.

14 A game: The shopping-trip

Divide the class into two teams. The team that gets the fewest penalty points is the winning team.

A **The careful housewives' team**

B **The rich husbands' team**

  a) Yesterday I went into town as usual and bought two eggs at the grocer's.
  b) Yesterday I went into town as usual and bought two eggs at the grocer's and several tins of fruit.
  c) Yesterday ..... and one bun at the baker's.
  d) Go on!

15 Sabine's English phrase-book

> Yesterday a girl stopped me in the street and said:
> "Hallo, don't I know you?"
> "I don't think so," I replied.
> "Don't you know me?" she cried.
> "I'm afraid I don't," I explained.
> "Never mind," she said. "It's a lovely day, isn't it?"
> "It certainly is. So long!"

16 Carsten's English scrapbook

The Thames is Britain's most famous river. Carsten has drawn a map of Britain. On it he has drawn the other big English and Scottish rivers: for example, the Severn and the Humber. London is Britain's most important port. There are several others. Can you put them on your map in your own scrapbook?

17 A proverb: Everybody's business is nobody's business.

18 A joke: Cannibal tourist from Africa: "I think your policemen are wonderful!"

Unit 14

A bird called Esmeralda

Step 1

Unit 14

A bird called Esmeralda

a) Look and listen
b) Look, listen and repeat

1 This bird is a budgie. | It has no freedom, | because it's in a cage.

2 The budgie is called Esmeralda. | She's very intelligent and can speak.

3 That budgie is useless. It can't speak.

4 The lady is opening the window | because the postman is knocking on it.

5 The budgie is flying out of the cage | because it wants a bit of freedom.

6 The budgie has flown into the house opposite. | It's sitting on the teapot now.

Step 2   "Rubbish!"

Carsten: 367 2264. Carsten speaking.
Lady: Are you the boy who lives opposite?
Carsten: I don't know. Who is speaking, please?
Lady: You must know who I am. I live opposite your house.
Carsten: Are you the lady who has the budgie?
Lady: Oh dear. Yes! You see, I'm telephoning because Esmeralda has disappeared.
Carsten: I don't understand. You keep the bird in a cage, don't you?

Lady: Not all the time. A bird which has no freedom can't be happy and sing well. I let Esmeralda fly around the dining-room. From twelve to one she can leave her cage and she comes and sits on my plate and eats a bit of my lunch and ... oh, dear, oh dear.

Carsten: But why did Esmeralda get out of the dining-room?

Lady: Because the postman arrived and knocked on the window, and because I opened it. Then the children who are always playing in the street called "Esmeralda!" and she flew out and ...

Carsten: Don't cry! I'll find your budgie for you. I'll tell the policeman who is always standing on the corner and I'll try all the neighbours. Can your budgie speak?

Lady: Of course. A budgie which can't speak is useless. Esmeralda is very intelligent. She can say "Rubbish!"

Carsten: And what else?

Lady: Isn't that enough? It's very good and very funny. It's very difficult for a budgie to say "Rubbish!"

Budgie: Rubbish, rubbish, rubbish!

Lady: What did you say?

Carsten: I didn't say anything, but there is a budgie sitting on the teapot.

Lady: Close all the doors and all the windows! I'm coming at once. We've found my darling Esmeralda!

Questions

a) Why doesn't the old lady tell Carsten her name?
   Where does the lady live?
   Why is the lady telephoning?
   Does she always keep the budgie in a cage?

b) Why does she let the budgie fly around the room?
   When can the budgie leave its cage?
   Where does the budgie sit?
   What does the budgie do on the plate?

c) Why did the budgie get out of the dining-room?
   Why did the lady open the window?
   Whom did Carsten want to try?
   Why is the budgie very intelligent?

d) Which word is very difficult for a budgie?
   Where is the budgie sitting now?
   What must Carsten do?
   What is the old lady going to do?

e) Why don't you do your homework at five o'clock in the morning?
   Why don't you like playing tennis in the middle of the night?

Why don't you feed your dog in the bathroom?
Why can't you buy cakes at the butcher's?
Why mustn't you eat chocolate in your English lesson?
Why mustn't you bring a dog to school?
What is the name of a man who brings letters?
What is the name of a man who drives a lorry?
What is the name of a man who milks cows?

Step 3 Drills in Drill Book 3, Unit 7

Step 4 "Pretty Joe!"

The English are very fond of animals. They love dogs, cats, and budgerigars, and a lot of English families have pets; but, unfortunately, dogs usually hate cats and cats usually hate birds. The story that follows is about a dog called Spot, a cat called Sam, and a budgie called Joe.

5 Joe was tired of his cage, which was too small, and he was tired of his owner, an old lady called Mrs. Hancock. He didn't like saying "Pretty Joe! Pretty Joe! Good morning! Good morning!" all day. Who wanted to do that? Certainly not Joe! "I'm an intelligent budgie," thought Joe; "and I'm tired of this awful old cage and this useless old woman. 'Pretty Joe! Good morning!' What rubbish!
10 What useless rubbish!"

Every Thursday afternoon Mrs. Hancock let Joe out of his cage, which was in the living-room, because she wanted to clean the cage. One Thursday someone knocked on the front-door. Mrs. Hancock left the room, and, because she forgot to shut the door, Joe was able to fly out of the living-room, through the open
15 front-door, and across the road to a tree which was in the garden opposite. "I'm free!" thought Joe. "And I shan't return! Ha ha! Won't she be angry!"

But Mrs. Hancock wasn't angry, because she forgot about Joe. She even forgot to clean his cage; instead she went into the kitchen to make tea.
Half an hour later it began to rain. Joe didn't like the rain, and he was hungry, and he was cold. "Why doesn't she come and look for me?" he thought. "I'll go and look." He flew to the window of Mrs. Hancock's living-room, but it was shut. "I'll wait on the windowsill," thought Joe. "I'm tired of the rain, and I'm tired of my freedom."
And then Sam appeared. Sam was the big black cat which lived next door, and Sam hated all birds: he liked to catch them and eat them. Sam saw Joe, and slowly, very slowly, he crept towards the window-sill . . .

And then Spot appeared! Spot lived in the house opposite, and he hated all cats, especially Sam, whom he often ran after. Sam saw Joe, and Spot saw Sam — and, just in time, Joe also saw Sam! Sam jumped at Joe, Joe flew into the air, and Spot raced across the road after Sam. The noise was awful!
At that moment Mrs. Hancock opened the front-door. Quickly, Joe flew into the house, into the living-room, and into his cage, the door of which was still open. Sam raced into the house after him, and Spot followed Sam: they knocked old Mrs. Hancock over. "Oh! Oh! You bad, bad animals!" she shouted.

Unit 14

There was a terrible noise in the living-room, and Sam and Spot raced out of the house — and knocked Mrs. Hancock over again. Mrs. Hancock got up slowly and went back into the house.

The mess in her living-room was awful. Her best teapot was in pieces on the
5 floor, and tea, milk, sugar, sandwiches and cake were everywhere. There was even a bit of cake, a large bit of cake, in Joe's cage. "Those naughty, bad animals!" said Mrs. Hancock. "Why did they come into the house? They didn't frighten you, Joe darling, did they? And — oh! — my poor teapot!"

Joe ate the bit of cake, the large bit of cake, that was in his cage. Joe liked cake.
10 Joe was very grateful to be in his cage again. "Good morning!" said Joe.

Step 5   1 Why was Joe tired of his cage? ●

2 Why did they do it?

Please ask questions with 'why' and answer them with 'because'.

Example: Sam approached the window-sill. Joe was sitting on it.
Why did Sam approach the window-sill?
Because Joe was sitting on it.

a) Joe was tired of Mrs. Hancock. She was a useless old woman.
b) Joe hated saying 'Good morning' all day. He was an intelligent bird.
c) Mrs. Hancock left the room. Someone was at the door.
d) Joe was very happy. He was really free.
e) Joe was unhappy. He didn't like rain.
f) Joe couldn't get into the living-room. The window was shut.
g) Joe flew up into the air. He saw Sam.
h) Joe could fly into the house. Mrs. Hancock opened her front-door.
i) Mrs. Hancock dropped the milk-bottle. Sam and Spot knocked her over.
j) Joe said "Good morning!" He was grateful to be in his cage again.

3 Conjunctions ★

4 Joe is tired of everything

Example: I am tired of this cage. You bought it three years ago.
I am tired of this cage **which** you bought three years ago.

a) I am tired of this cake. You bought it last week.
b) I am tired of your old records. You got them ten years ago.
c) I am tired of these pictures. You bought them five years ago.
d) I am tired of these biscuits. You got them a month ago.
e) I am tired of this silly cat. It chases birds.
f) I am tired of this teapot. It is much too big.
g) I am tired of this house. It is much too small.
h) I am tired of this room. It is much too noisy.
i) I am tired of the goldfish. They are much too tasteless.
j) I am tired of the television. It is much too boring.

5 Useful verbs which we must remember. Can you form a sentence with each?

	today	yesterday
to shut	he shuts	he shut
to let	he lets	he let
to leave	he leaves	he left
to drop	he drops	he dropped
to stop	he stops	he stopped
to drive	he drives	he drove
to find	he finds	he found
to forget	he forgets	he forgot
to think	he thinks	he thought
to pay	he pays	he paid
to fly	he flies	he flew
to be able	he can	he could

6 Here is a very sad story

Mrs. Dinsdale forgets to shut the cage.
Bobo the budgie flies out.
He leaves the room through the open window.
He thinks it is wonderful to be free!
A baker drops a piece of cake.
Bobo sees the piece of cake in the road.
A car comes, but the driver can't stop.
He drives over Bobo's left leg.
The driver lets Bobo lie there.
Mrs. Dinsdale finds him.

Please tell this sad story again. Begin: Last Thursday Mrs. Dinsdale **forgot** to shut the cage. Bobo . . . .

7 Can you say who is what?

A bird-lover is somebody who is fond of birds.

And a cat-lover?
A dog-lover?
An animal-lover?

A woman-hater is somebody who hates women.

And a man-hater?
A child-hater?
A lady-hater?

A postman is somebody who brings letters to your house.
A porter (to carry suitcases): A porter is somebody . . .

A bus-driver	(to drive a bus):		
A dentist	(to pull out teeth):	A farmer	(to milk cows):
A teacher	(to give lessons):	A milkman	(to deliver milk):
A policeman	(to stop robbers):	A reporter	(to write for newspapers):
A paper-boy	(to deliver papers):	A tourist	(to take photographs):

Unit 14

8 Your job is to find the right adjectives ■

9 Who can write down the most sentences in the shortest time?

Perhaps this is I shan't talk to	the lady the boy the burglar the girl the fool	who	whispered at the back. stole my handbag. lost my key. took my photograph. gave me the bad egg.
	the pupil the assistant	whose	father won the match. sister is flying to Berlin. parents have gone to Bonn.
Here is a description of This is a photograph of The postman brought me a letter about	something	which that	you will think important. will be useful.

10 Which do you like best? ●

11 Which is more intelligent? A test ● ■ ★

12 What is wrong? Correct these sentences, please.

```
A purse            is a shop in which we can buy cakes.
A swan             is a boat which pulls barges.
A budgie           is a book in which we write our adventures.
An athletics match is something that you must buy before going on a train.
A good memory      is a competition in which we run and jump.
A ticket           is a bird which swims on the river.
A diary            is a small bag in which we carry money.
A tug              is something which we all must have.
A baker's shop     is a bird which can talk.
```

13 Proverbs

It is a long lane that has no turning.
It is the last straw that breaks the camel's back.
Don't bite the hand that feeds you.

14 A guessing game: What is my job?

One pupil chooses a job, but he doesn't say what it is. He or she must answer the questions of the rest of the class. He may answer only with "yes" or "no". After ten questions (or after two wrong guesses) the pupil has beaten the class. You can choose a job from this list: postman, doctor, porter, shop-assistant, dentist, grocer, butcher, baker, greengrocer, farmer, bus-driver, bank robber, milkman. There are, of course, many other jobs which you can choose.

Here are some examples of questions which are useful for this game:

Are you a man who stands behind a counter?
Are you a girl who works in a shop?
Is your work mostly outside?
Do you stand up when you are working?
Do you wear a uniform for work?
Do you work with your hands?
Do you make something?
Can we eat what you make?
Do you help other people?

15 Sabine's English phrase-book

> I met an American lady <u>the other day</u>.
> I told her the way to Buckingham Palace and she thanked me, and I said, "<u>Don't mention it</u>."
> Then she gave me a little book about New York, and I thanked her, and she said, "<u>You're welcome</u>."
> "You're welcome" is American for "Don't mention it".
> Are these two different languages? I hope not.

Unit 15

Stuck in a snowdrift

Step 1

Unit 15

Stuck in a snowdrift

a) Look and listen
b) Look, listen and repeat

1 When you have strong winds | and a lot of snow, | you have a blizzard. | We had a blizzard last week.

2 On the way home from school, | the school bus stuck in a snowdrift.

3 The teacher, old Miss Ponsonby, | tried to walk through the blizzard | to the nearest telephone.

4 But Miss Ponsonby fell and broke both her legs.

5 When she didn't return, | Roger Higgins went through the snowdrift | and walked to the nearest hospital.

6 The doctor at the hospital | came with an ambulance | and rescued Miss Ponsonby.

Step 2   **An exciting trip to hospital**

Carsten: If you don't give me something to eat, I'll never speak to you again! I haven't eaten anything for 12 hours!
Sabine: There isn't anything in the larder. I'm very sorry.
Carsten: Haven't you got some cake or some biscuits in the kitchen?
Sabine: Nothing at all.
Carsten: Aren't there any apples?
Sabine: Stop thinking about food. Think of poor Mummy, because she's out there in all that snow. We're all right — we're warm and safe.

Carsten: Warm and safe? Hah! Warm and hungry!

Sabine: If the snowplough can reach us, you'll be able to go to the shops and buy something to eat.

Carsten: If, if, if! Look out of the window, my dear sister. Can you see any snowploughs? Of course you can't. The snow is still falling, and snowdrifts are blocking our front-door. Wait a minute. I can hear something. What can it be?

Sabine: The snowplough.

Carsten: This time you're right. It really is a snowplough. And behind it there's a police car. I'll stop it if I can.

Sabine: It's all right. It's stopping here.

Policeman: Good afternoon, Miss. Are you Sabine Grau whose mother fell downstairs this morning and broke both her legs?

Sabine: Is she O. K.? Did my father reach Ramsgate hospital?

Policeman: No, he didn't. His car stuck in a snowdrift a mile from the hospital. He had to get out and walk.

Carsten: Oh no! And my poor mother?

Policeman: He had to leave her in the car. When he reached the hospital, he got in an ambulance and tried to go back to your mother. But the snowdrifts were too bad. Nobody does anything at all when the weather is so bad. I always say . . .

Sabine: My mother, where is my mother now?

Policeman: Don't worry, Miss. She's safe and sound in hospital. She'll be all right.

Carsten: How did she reach the hospital, if the ambulance also stuck in a snowdrift?

Policeman: That's quite simple, sonny. When the ambulance returned without your mother, the people at the hospital telephoned the R.A.F. They asked them for a helicopter because no ambulance could reach your mother.

Carsten: Did the helicopter have any trouble?

Policeman: No, everything was all right. The helicopter flew to your mother and rescued her. You can read everything in tomorrow's paper.

Sabine: If there is a paper tomorrow.

Carsten: If we can reach a shop and buy a paper tomorrow.

Policeman: Well, I must go. Is there anything you want?

Carsten: Have you some nice egg sandwiches? You haven't? Can we come with you to the nearest food shop? Can you take us in your car? I must eat something.

Policeman: Are you hungry, sonny? All right, jump in.

Questions

a) Why is Carsten so hungry? *He hasn't eaten anything for 12 hours*
Why can't Carsten have anything to eat? *There isn't anything in the larder*
What has Sabine got to eat in the kitchen? *She has nothing to eat in the kitchen*

b) Why must Carsten think of his poor mother? *Because she is out in all that snow*
Why must Carsten and Sabine be grateful? *They are warm and safe*
Does Carsten feel warm and safe? *No he doesn't. He feels warm and hungry*
When will Carsten get something to eat?
Is the sun shining? *No it isn't*

c) What is stopping outside Carsten's window? *A policecar is stopping outside*
What happened to Sabine's mother?
Why didn't Sabine's father reach the hospital? *He is stuck in a snowdrift a mile from the Hospital*
What did Mr. Grau do next?
What happened to Mr. Grau's wife? *She fell downstairs this morning and broke both her legs*

d) Did the ambulance reach Mrs. Grau? *No it didn't*
What do people do when the weather is really bad?
Where was the ambulance stuck? *It stuck in a snowdrift.*
What did the people at the hospital do next? *They telephoned the RAF*
Why did they ask for a helicopter? *Because no ambulance could reach Mrs Grau*

e) Where did the helicopter fly to? *It flew to Mrs. Grau.*
Where could Carsten read about it? *He could read it in the paper*
Was there anything Carsten wanted?
Did the policemen have any room in their car? *Yes they did*

Questions which only you can answer.

Is there anything you want at this moment?
Do you want anything to eat, or to drink?
Have you eaten anything since breakfast?
Will you have something to eat when you arrive home after school?
Did you have any English homework for today?
Have you got any favourite flowers, animals, pictures?
Have you got some nice pictures in your bedroom?
What will you do if you ever see an accident?
What must you do when you see a person lying in the snow?
What can't you do when you have broken both your legs?
What is a car called which takes people to hospital?

Step 3 Drills in Drill Book 3, Unit 8

A   The newspaper report

The Morning News
Monday, 27th March

SNOW AND STRONG WINDS IN SOUTH
Blizzard blocks roads.

A lot of snow fell in the south of England last night and is still falling. Strong winds have caused big snowdrifts which have blocked many roads.

"The roads are very bad," say the police "— there hasn't been anything like it in March for twenty years. Snowploughs are busy, but if the blizzard doesn't stop soon, there won't be any roads at all that the snow hasn't blocked."

By midnight some towns had ten inches of snow. Drivers had to leave their cars and walk home. In Kent and Sussex a lot of people could not leave their houses because snowdrifts blocked their front-doors.

Helicopter rescue: woman unconscious in car

An R.A.F. helicopter made an exciting rescue early this morning. A German family — Mr. and Mrs. Grau, and their children, Sabine and Carsten, who are living in England for a year — visited some friends near Ramsgate for the weekend. Late last night Mrs. Grau fell down the stairs in her friends' house and broke both her legs. Mr. Grau tried to drive her to Ramsgate hospital, but his car stuck in a snowdrift a mile from the hospital. Mr. Grau had to leave his wife in the car and walk. He reached the hospital two hours later.

An ambulance that went to fetch Mrs. Grau also stuck in a snowdrift, and so the hospital telephoned the R.A.F. and asked them to deal with the situation. They offered to send a helicopter, but the wind and snow were so bad that at first the pilot could not find the Graus' car. When he at last saw it, it was almost under the snow, and Mrs. Grau was unconscious. She was still unconscious when she arrived at the hospital, five hours later.

Woman very ill

A doctor at the hospital said in an interview: "Mrs. Grau is very ill, but if she is lucky she will be all right." And he added: "I am very angry. Mrs. Grau almost died. It is always the same when there is any snow: the snow always blocks the roads, and no-one is able to drive safely. Why doesn't someone do something about the roads as soon as snow falls? Why do careless drivers go so fast? I have a lot of useful suggestions which I'm going to send to my M.P."

B The reporter's story

Tuesday, 28th March

Reporter: Mr. Grau, did you worry when your car stuck in that snowdrift?
Mr. Grau: Yes, of course. My wife was in great pain, and the children were alone in the house.
Reporter: Was the snow very deep?
5 *Mr. Grau:* Yes, and I didn't have any boots. My feet got very wet and cold, and after ten minutes they began to hurt a lot. And it snowed all the time, and I couldn't see.
Reporter: Carsten, were you and Sabine all right? Did you worry?
Carsten: No, we didn't worry very much. But we got rather hungry because
10 there wasn't much food in the house — and we also got very thirsty, as all the water froze.
Reporter: Weren't you cold?
Sabine: No — we went to bed and stayed there. It was the warmest place in the house.
15 *Reporter:* Didn't anything frighten you?
Sabine: Well — our mother's broken legs did. We worried about that.
Carsten: And we were alone for a long time.
Sabine: And it was very dark outside. I couldn't see any lights, and there wasn't a sound.
20 *Reporter:* Thank you. That will make a useful story for my newspaper. I must go now: I have to drive to Brighton, in Sussex.
Mr. Grau: Good-bye.
Reporter: Good-bye. Oh! How is Mrs. Grau? Is she still very ill?
Mr. Grau: No, she is much better, but she'll have to stay in hospital for several
25 more days.
Reporter: What a pity! There isn't a story in that, is there? Never mind! But, if she gets worse, you will telephone me and tell me, won't you? Good-bye!

1 Carsten is very hungry

Carsten has come back from a very long walk and is terribly hungry. So he asks his mother: Is there **any** pudding in the house?

His mother replies: Sorry, **there isn't any** pudding, but there is **some** delicious cake.

Please go on asking Carsten's questions and giving his mother's answers. Use some of these words: marmalade, jam, bread and butter, ice-cream, chocolate cake, pie, Irish Stew, meat, sausage, fish.

2 I'm afraid there isn't any bacon either ■

3 Carsten wants to get back to London ★

4 Lunch with Mother

Please fill in 'some' or 'any':

Barry: Sorry, Mum, I can't eat — more potatoes.
Mother: That's all right, Barry.
 Will you have — more meat?
Barry: No thanks. May I have — tomatoes?
Mother: I'm afraid there aren't —.
Barry: Didn't you buy — on Thursday?
Mother: No, I didn't get —.
Barry: Then I'll have — tea, please. Is there — pudding?
Mother: No, there isn't — pudding, but there is — nice fruit cake.
Barry: Wonderful. I'll have —.

5 Roger the runner hasn't got many books ●

6 Ask the pupil beside you questions, but choose the right preposition carefully

Have you got anything Is there anything	interesting exciting attractive useful expensive delicious funny	in on under	your diary? your pocket? your desk? your window-sill? your English book? your chair? your handbag?
Did you	buy enjoy hear see hear of take a photograph of get information on	any new records any good books any interesting films any runners any handsome film stars any modern pictures
any famous men
any high buildings	last week? last month? last year? when you were in Paris? in Paris? in London? the other day?

Unit 15

Which words are not right in these lists?
a) Swan, budgie, cow, hour, horse, cat, dog.
b) Tug, boat, train, cage, bike, helicopter, ambulance.

7 Tom's form master is very cross

Tom is doing everything wrong, but he always has some excuse. Can you find the best excuses for these questions and use the word 'because'?

Form Master:	*Tom:*
Why did you arrive late this morning?	I had no more writing paper.
Why didn't you finish your homework?	It was too cold.
Why didn't you bring any money for our trip?	I was so hot.
Why didn't you drink your milk at break?	My mother forgot to call me.
Why did you come without a coat?	I lost my purse.
Why haven't you got a history book?	I left my bag on the kitchen table.

8 When I have finished: Oliver's afternoon

Example: Tom: What do you do when you have finished school? (to go home)
  Oliver: When I have finished school, I go home.

a) What do you do when you have arrived home? (to have tea)
b) What do you do when you have finished tea? (to start my homework)
c) What do you do when you have finished your homework? (to do some shopping)
d) What do you do when you have finished your shopping? (to visit a friend)
e) What do you do when you have returned home? (to have supper)
f) What do you do when you have had supper? (to watch television)
g) What do you do when you have watched television? (to have a cup of hot milk)
h) What do you do when you have had your hot milk? (to wash in the bathroom)
i) What do you do when you have washed? (to go to bed)

9 What sort of weather do you like? ● ■ ★

10 What will you do if that happens?

Example: Alan: I hope I'll get a good report.
  Tom: What will you do if you get a good report?

Please go on and ask questions and use 'if':
a) I hope I'll get a new camera.
b) I hope I'll get some more pocket money.
c) I hope I'll meet Joan.
d) I hope I'll see John in the holidays.
e) I hope I'll get a job in the holidays.
f) I hope I'll have good weather at the weekend.
g) I hope I'll play in the big match.
h) I hope I'll find a pen-friend next term.

Now write down the answers to these questions. Start with the word 'if'.

For example: Here is the answer to a): If I get a new camera, I'll take lots of photographs.

11 A new comprehensive school ■

12 Word-building ★

13 We write a story

Use these words and write a story about "The Budgie and the Silly Old Cow".

a) Something funny, sad, exciting, unusual
b) to happen to me, to my aunt, to my uncle, to my friend
c) last week, last Tuesday, the day before yesterday, last night.
d) To go upstairs after watching television and to see a budgie, to sit
e) on the bed, table, under the chair.
f) The green and blue bird to say: "Silly old cow! How are you?"
g) To close the window and to take the bird into the bathroom.
h) To hurry downstairs and to telephone the police, but police to be very sorry and to have no time. To wait until morning.
i) Next morning to go to bathroom. Budgie to say "good night!"
j) Old lady to knock at front-door. To ask about budgie. To be the owner. To go and get a cage.
k) Old lady to be very happy. To pay big reward. Budgie to say to her: 'Silly old cow' and old lady to smile happily. To say "Very clever bird. My greatest friend!"

14 A limerick

There was a young student in Crete
Who stood on his head in the street.
He said, "It is clear,
If I want to stay here,
I shall have to shake hands with my feet."

15 A competition: True or False?

a) Glasgow is an English county.
b) Hull lies at the mouth of the river Humber.
c) Cardiff is the biggest city in Wales.
d) Liverpool is a fine town in Ireland.
e) London buses are yellow or blue.
f) A London policeman is called a Billy.
g) A swan is a bird.
h) The English children's school-day ends at a quarter past three.
i) Birmingham is four hundred miles north of London.
j) There are three terms in a school year.

You will find the answers on page 169

16 Sabine's English phrase-book

> We have had some very bad weather.
> Last week we had a <u>snowstorm</u>.
> Last Monday there was <u>ice</u> on the road.
> Last Tuesday there was a lot of <u>fog</u>.
> Last Wednesday <u>it poured with rain</u>.
> Last Thursday we had <u>gales</u> blowing across the British Isles.
> And today another <u>low</u> is coming from the west and moving East towards Germany.

17 Carsten's English scrapbook

The English are great dog-lovers. But sometimes they lose their dogs. Then policemen take these lost dogs to the oldest and most famous dogs' home in the world — the Battersea Dogs Home in London. Last year, 16,000 dogs arrived there. Some owners never come to fetch their dogs, but most of them do.
The English are excellent dog-breeders and export dogs to all parts of the world. Are you interested in dogs? Why not find out some of the names of typical English dogs?

18 English customs

On Good Friday, the Friday before Easter Sunday, the English eat hot Cross Buns with a lot of butter. They are buns with the sign of the cross on them. On Easter Sunday the English wish each other "Happy Easter!" and eat eggs for breakfast. The children have drawn faces on them and have coloured them in different colours, just as you do.

Unit 16

Going by tube

Step 1

1

2

3

4

5

6

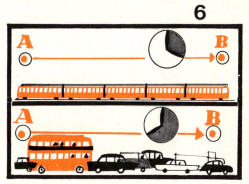

Unit 16

Going by tube

a) Look and listen
b) Look, listen and repeat

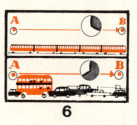

1 This is a map of the London Underground or Tube. | There are eight different lines.

2 Many Londoners go by tube to the West End.

3 There are many big department stores | and theatres in the West End.

4 If you have some small change | you can get your ticket from a ticket machine.

5 If you want a cheap meal in the West End | you must go to a self-service restaurant.

6 Going by tube is the fastest way. | A tube train takes only twenty minutes | when a bus takes forty minutes for the same journey.

Step 2

The underground

Angela: It's my birthday next Tuesday. Can you come with me to the theatre? I'm going to see the new play at the Haymarket Theatre.
Sabine: Yes, I can. Thanks a lot!
Angela: Wonderful. Let's go and get the tickets now.
Sabine: How do you get to the Haymarket. By bus?
Angela: No, it's much quicker by tube. The trains run every few minutes and are very fast.
Sabine: I don't like the tube — it frightens me: there are so many platforms, and I always lose my way.

Angela: Don't be silly! It's quite easy. Look — here's a map of the London Underground at the back of my diary. There are eight lines, and each line is a different colour on the map.

Sabine: Yes, I see. But then there are the ticket-machines. I don't understand them. They never give me the right ticket.

Angela: Well, you can buy your ticket at the ticket-office, if you want to. If you have no small change, you must also go to the ticket-office. You give the man your money, and he gives you the right ticket. It's easy!

Sabine: Yes, but things can still go wrong. They went wrong last week when Carsten and I went to the West End. We wanted to go to Oxford Circus and then to visit some department stores and have a meal at a self-service restaurant. We went by Tube from Charing Cross, and it took us an hour to get there.

Angela: An hour from Charing Cross to Oxford Circus? I can't believe it! Nonsense! It takes only six minutes.

Sabine: Ah, but you're a Londoner and know the Underground well. After getting the tickets we went to the wrong platform, and got on a train on the wrong line. We had to get out at the next station and catch a train back to Charing Cross.

Angela: And that took you a whole hour?

Sabine: No, it didn't. But at Charing Cross we got the wrong train again.

Angela: How did you do that?

Sabine: A very kind gentleman told us the way to the right platform. But unfortunately he didn't know the Tube well either. We caught the wrong train again and didn't reach Oxford Circus until just before five thirty.

Angela: So you were too late for the shops?

Sabine: Much too late, I'm afraid. But we went to a self-service restaurant and had a delicious meal. Then we went home.

Angela: By Tube, I hope. It really is the best and fastest way.

Sabine: No, we walked. That's the safest way!

Questions and answers

1 What does Angela want to do on her birthday?
2 How often do the Tube trains run?
3 Why does Sabine always lose her way in the Underground?
4 Why does Sabine hate the ticket-machines?
5 What do you have to do when you have no small change?
6 Why did Sabine have to get out at the next station?
7 When did they finally reach Oxford Circus?
8 What did they do then?

Step 3 Drills in Drill Book 3, Unit 9

Step 4 Sabine's Diary:

A **A meal on a tray**

London, 3rd May

Daddy is a person who likes to plan everything very carefully. The day before yesterday he told Carsten and me: "As you know, tomorrow is your mother's birthday. Before you say anything, let me explain: your mother has worked much too hard in the last few weeks and has had little or no free time. So on her
5 birthday I'm going to take her to a good restaurant and to the opera — alone. No cooking for her tomorrow. Carsten and you can get a meal in a self-service restaurant in the West End. And after looking at the shops you can use these tickets. Yes, they are tickets for the Covent Garden Opera House, but you won't be very near us. Your mother and I have tickets for the tenth row in the Stalls.
10 Your seats are high up in the Upper Circle. But you must promise to go straight home after the opera. It's a modern opera by the British composer Benjamin Britten."

So yesterday afternoon Carsten and I went by tube to Piccadilly Circus. The London underground trains run every few minutes and are very fast. It took us
15 only fifteen minutes to the West End. We walked down Regent Street, turned into Oxford Street and finally went into Selfridges, a big department store. Carsten went round to the record department while I had a good look at the summer dresses. After spending about an hour in the store we went to "Meal on a Tray", a self-service restaurant in Oxford Street. There are no waitresses
20 there. After taking a tray, you go along a counter and choose as much or as little as you want to eat. Carsten took a plate of fish cakes and chips, and a pudding, while I chose mushroom soup and a steak-and-kidney pie. I also took a cup of hot milk; Carsten chose a cup of cocoa. Before paying at the cash desk at the end of the counter we each took a paper serviette, and a knife, fork and
25 spoon. Then we carried our meals on a tray to a table. Everything was still beautifully hot. We didn't have to wait for a busy waitress and we found the meal very tasty and quite cheap.

Questions about "A meal on a tray"

a) Why does Sabine's mother need a rest?
b) Why can't Carsten eat at home on his mother's birthday?
c) Did Carsten and his sister sit near their parents?
d) Are the seats in the Upper Circle more expensive than seats in the stalls?
e) How do you get from Piccadilly Circus to Oxford Street?
f) How is a self-service restaurant different from another restaurant?
g) Why did Sabine like the self-service restaurant?

1 The old corner shop hasn't much to sell ●   Step 5

2 Too much of it is a nuisance

Bob: **A little** rain can be nice.
Paul: Yes, but **too much of it** is a nuisance.
Please go on with: freedom, free time, snow, hot sunshine, rain, loud music.

3 We write lots of sentences about London

When I	come to	London	I	must see	the Tower.
If you ever	visit	England	you		Westminster Abbey.
When you	have a look at	Britain			the Houses of
While you	have a holiday in	the capital			Parliament.
					London Bridge.
					the Port of London.

4 Do your best

Eric: What do you want to do when you leave school, Brian?
Brian: I want to become a crane-driver.
Eric: Brian wants to become a crane-driver, Dad!
Father: If he does his best, he'll become a crane-driver.

Eric: Brian wants to become a teacher.
Father: If he . . . . .
Eric: Brian wants to become a postman.
         Brian wants to become a police inspector.
         Brian wants to become a farmer.
         Brian wants to become a baker.
         Brian wants to become a fisherman.
         Sheila wants to become a waitress.
         Sheila wants to become a shop assistant.

5 Which is the right word? Who or whose or whom or to whom?

Find the right word and then answer the question:
a) — did you meet at the corner today?
b) — did your headmaster send your school report?

c) — palace is called Buckingham Palace?
d) — did the budgie say 'Good morning!'?
e) — knocked over the teapot?
f) — memory was awful?

6 What do you have to do if somebody is very ill?

If somebody is very ill, I have to call the doctor.
What do you have to do:

a) if someone is shouting "Fire! Help!"?
b) if someone has no money for the bus?
c) if someone has seen a burglar in your house?
d) if someone has given you a marvellous present?
e) if someone speaks English too quickly?
f) if someone has lost his way?
g) if someone attacks your mother?
h) if you see an accident in the street?

7 At the hospital

8 What do you do when you have got up?

Example: John has got up. He washes.
When John has got up, he washes.

a) John has washed. He dresses.
b) He has dressed. He puts on his shoes.
c) He has put on his shoes. He goes downstairs.
d) He has gone downstairs. He has breakfast.
e) He has had breakfast. He says good-bye.
f) He has said good-bye. He goes to school.
g) He has gone to school. He begins lessons.
h) He has begun lessons. He listens carefully.

9 I enjoy cycling ★

10 But there weren't any more

You have to think quickly in this game. The teacher divides the class into two teams, the husbands and the wives.

Teacher: I needed some more eggs, but there weren't any more.
1st pupil in the Husbands' Team: I needed some more **lemons**, but there weren't any more.
1st pupil in the Wives' Team: I needed some more **tomatoes**, but there weren't any more.

Each team member has to think of a new word. If he doesn't do so in 10 seconds his team gets a penalty point.

11 Word-building: -ful and -less

When something is no good for anything, it is **useless**.
But when it is rather helpful, it is **useful**.
When something gives you a lot of pain, it is **painful**.
But when it doesn't give you any pain, it is **painless**.
When someone thinks a lot about other people, he is **thoughtful**.
When he doesn't think about the other people, he is **thoughtless**.
When someone is afraid, he is **fearful**.
When someone isn't afraid of anything, he is **fearless**.
Can you say what a **noiseless** car is? What is a **forgetful** boy?

12 What is a budgie?

Please explain these words in English.

Example: A budgie is a small bird. (to talk)
         A budgie is a small bird which can talk.

A swan is a big white bird. (to swim)
A cow is a black and white animal. (to give milk)
A tug is a small boat. (to pull big boats)
A washing-machine is a machine. (to wash a lot of shirts)
A cargo-ship is a ship. (to bring bananas from Africa)
A camera is a little box. (to take photographs)

13,1 Do you know the opposites?

The opposite of intelligent is stupid.
What are the opposites of: difficult? boring? a bit? north? bad? to leave? uninteresting?

13,2 A vocabulary competititon

Who can write down the most words about:

a) Rivers and Ports?
b) Farms?
c) A Party?

13,3 Can you pronounce these words correctly?

Please write two lists. In the first list you write all words which have the sound [au]. In the second list you put all words with the sound [əu]. Here are some examples of words with these sounds: cow, know, flower, show, now, tower, owner, window, grocer.

14 Can you tell this story?

1 Last — the Clarks (to go) to —, and the weather was —.
2 They (to come home) at — and it was already quite dark. Poor Mr. Clark (to be unable to) find his front-door key. He (to search) all his pockets but —.

3 His wife (to look) in her —. Young Jimmy Clark (to try) to climb in through the —. But it was —.
4 So finally Mr. Clark — the fire-brigade. It arrived after —.
5 The — had a big axe and (to smash) —.
6 They (to leave) the house very dirty. Poor Mrs. Clarke —.
7 Mrs. Clarke (to have to) clean the hall. Mr. Clark (to begin) to repair the —.
8 Then Mr. Clark (to decide) to drive the car into the garage. (to sit) in the car on something hard. Of course. It was —.

15 Can you be an interpreter for a German tourist who can't speak English?

Hotel Porter: Good evening, sir. What can I do for you?
Interpreter: Guten Abend . . . . .
German tourist: Ich brauche ein Zimmer für zwei Nächte.
Interpreter: I . . . . .
Hotel Porter: With one or with two beds?
Interpreter: Mit . . . . .
German tourist: Ein bequemes Bett. Darf ich meinen Hund ins Zimmer nehmen?
Interpreter: One . . . . .
Hotel Porter: Unfortunately that is impossible. Where is your luggage, sir?
Interpreter: Leider . . . . .
German tourist: Draußen in meinem Auto. Es steht auf der linken Seite des Parkplatzes.
Interpreter: Outside . . . . .

Hotel Porter: Our boy will fetch your suitcases at once, sir.
Interpreter: Unser . . . . .
German tourist: Ist das Zimmer sehr laut? Ich schlafe nicht gut.
Interpreter: Is the . . . . .
Hotel Porter: You will find the room very quiet.
Interpreter: Sie werden . . . . .

German tourist: Wann kann ich Abendbrot bekommen?
Interpreter: When . . . . .
Hotel Porter: The dining-room will be open at a quarter past seven, sir. Here is your key, sir.
Interpreter: Der Sp . . . . .
German tourist to interpreter: Herzlichen Dank. Sie haben sehr gut übersetzt.
Hotel Porter: What did he say?
Interpreter: He said: . . . . .

16 A joke

London policemen are polite, but London newspaper boys are not so polite. The other day a tourist in a German car opened his window and asked a newspaper boy: Which is the best way to the Tower of London? The boy answered: Shoot Prince Philip!

17 Sabine's English phrase-book

Woman: Show me **some** ties, please.
Shop assistant: What colour do you want?
Woman: Oh, **any colour**.
No, I don't like **any of these**.
Shop assistant: This tie is very nice. It costs only 25 pence.
Woman: Is there **something wrong** with it?
Shop assistant: Of course not, Madam.
Woman: No, **it isn't any good. In any case,** my husband doesn't want another tie for his birthday. Good morning.
Shop assistant: (After the woman has gone): **Some people** are quite impossible.

18 Test your honesty   Are you a really honest boy or girl?

You can find out. Just answer these questions:

a) Do you ever copy your homework from a neighbour?
(Never: 5 points; sometimes: 6 points; often: 2 points)

b) Are you ever late in the morning?
(Never: 2 points; sometimes: 5 points; often: 3 points)

c) You find a purse at a bus-stop. What do you do?
Do you 1 leave it where it is? or 2 take it to a police-station? or 3 put it in your pocket?
1 = 3 points, 2 = 5 points, 3 = 1 point

d) An awful old aunt comes and visits your mother and invites you to tea for the next Sunday.
Do you say 1 Sorry, I already have an invitation; or 2 I don't like you, or 3 Thank you very much, I'll come?
1 = 1 point, 2 = 3 points, 3 = 5 points

e) You see a woman in a shop stealing a nice new coat.
Do you 1 tell her to put the coat back; 2 shout loudly 'stop thief!'; or 3 look the other way?
1 = 5 points, 2 = 3 points and 3 = 1 point

Have you got 27 points? Then you can't add up.
The maximum is 26 points. If you have 26 points you are a very honest person.
If you get 17 points, you are still fairly honest.
If you get fewer than 10 points you sometimes lie.

19 Audio-lingual comprehension dialogue: Is there anything to eat? ■

Unit 17

A plane is on fire!

Step 1

1

2

3

4

5

6

Unit 17

A plane is on fire!

a) Look and listen
b) Look, listen and repeat

Television Reporter:

1   I'm standing here on the Roof Gardens of London Airport. | I think the plane with Julia Himmelreich, | the great film star, | will arrive in two minutes.

Television reporter:

2   Ah yes, here is the British European Airways jet | with our dear Julia. | It's starting to land now. No! Oh no!!

Television reporter:

3   This is terrible. The whole plane is on fire! | But the plane has landed | and the passengers as well as the stewardesses | are jumping out.

Television reporter:

4   Ambulances and fire-engines | are going out to the burning plane. We are getting a very good view from up here. | But where is Julia?

Announcer:

5   Attention please: | All passengers on this jet from New York are safe and sound, | but the departure of the Scandinavian Airline jet | will be ten minutes late.

Television reporter:

6   Here is our Julia now. | She is coming up the escalator to the cafeteria. | She's got sun-glasses on. | She's smiling. No, she's crying. | Miss Himmelreich, what about your trip?

Good-byes at London Airport

Step 2

Carsten: We have arrived at the airport much too early. Now we'll have to wait a whole hour before our plane leaves.

Sabine: I was afraid of missing the plane. Must we say good-bye to Jill and Julia now?

Carsten: No, we needn't. We've lots of time. We can all go up to the Roof Gardens. They are open to visitors as well as passengers. From there we can watch all the planes landing and taking off.

Jill: That's a good idea! But what about your luggage?

Carsten: We haven't got much luggage. Daddy has sent all the bigger things to Germany by ship. Come on, we can go up on this escalator.

Julia: What a wonderful view! Just look at all those planes! Are you going by Lufthansa German airlines?

Sabine: No, we're going by British European Airways. All seats on German planes were booked.

Jill: Look at that big plane on the left! It's going to take off!

Announcer: The plane which is taking off now is the Scandinavian Airline Jet to New York via the North Pole. Attention please! Italian Airlines announce the departure of their Flight Number 167 for Rome. Passengers for this flight, please go to gate number 11.

Sabine: I think I've seen enough. I must have a last cup of English tea before leaving.

Jill: Well, there are plenty of shops as well as a cafeteria at the airport. It's a small town, you know, with banks, a police-station, and an animal hotel.

Carsten: You and your stories!

Jill: Don't be silly! I read about it last week. The animals arrive here and have a rest before flying on to other airports.

Julia: Wait a minute. Here's a shop with picture postcards. I want to buy some for my little brother.

Jill: And I need a pair of sun-glasses.

Sabine: Get me a box of English chocolates, please, Carsten. I must take something English for our friends in Germany.

Announcer: Passengers for BEA flight 421 for Cologne, please go to gate 9.

Carsten: Well, this is it. We must say our good-byes now.

Sabine: Thank you very much for showing me so much of London, you two!

Jill: Here are some strawberries for eating on the flight.

Carsten: Thank you very much for everything!

Julia: Don't forget to write. Have a good trip!

Sabine: Don't forget to come and visit us in Germany!

Carsten: Remember, it's only one hour and ten minutes by plane!

Questions

1. How long will they have to wait before their plane leaves?
2. Why haven't they got much luggage?
3. Why aren't they going by Lufthansa Airlines?
4. How is the plane going to New York?
5. What does Sabine want to do before leaving?
6. What do the animals do at the animal hotel?
7. What does Sabine want to take for her friends in Germany?
8. How long does it take to fly from London to Cologne?

Step 3 Drills in Drill Books 3, Unit 10

Step 4 Sabine's Diary: Fasten your seat belts!

12th July

Our year in England is over, and I have come to the end of my diary. Yesterday afternoon we said our good-byes to the neighbours, locked the front-door of our flat in Surbiton and took a taxi to London Airport. My friend Jill and Carsten's friend Julia met us there. We were much too early and had a whole
5 hour before the departure of our plane. Fortunately we didn't have much luggage as Daddy had sent all the bigger things by ship. He is staying another week in England, while Mummy went back to Cologne a week ago to get our flat ready. So we didn't have more than a small suitcase each and were able to go up on the escalator to the Roof Gardens. As they are also open to visitors, Jill and Julia
10 were able to come with us.

It was a fine, sunny day and we had a wonderful view from up there. We saw lots of planes landing and taking off. Over 800 planes arrive or leave here every

day of the week, a stewardess told me later. London airport has five runways. The longest is 12,000 feet. I had my camera with me and took a picture of an intercontinental airliner when it took off for New York via the North Pole. We also saw a German Airlines Lufthansa jet from Hamburg. We were not able to get seats on a Lufthansa plane as all seats on German planes were already booked. The month of July is the beginning of the summer holidays. But we got very good seats on a fast British European Airways plane to Cologne, which can fly there in just over an hour.

I didn't want to leave England without having a last cup of English tea, so we all went to the big airport cafeteria. But Carsten wasn't thirsty and had a look at the airport's animal hotel. The thousands of animals which arrive at the airport every year can have a rest there before flying on to other parts of Europe. Some only stay for a drink and a few hours' rest; others stay for several days until their new owners collect them. Carsten saw not only fish and birds, but also monkeys, snakes and even elephants.

Later I went to a shop inside the airport and spent my last English money on a pair of sun-glasses, half a dozen picture-postcards and a box of English chocolates for our friends in Cologne. Jill bought me some strawberries for eating on the flight, and then came the loudspeaker message:

"Attention please. British European Airways announce the departure of their flight number 421 for Cologne. Passengers for this flight, please go to gate number 9!"

It was time to say our good-byes. I thanked Jill and Julia for showing us so much of London and asked them to visit us in Cologne. Then we walked out to our plane, while Jill and Julia hurried up to the Roof Gardens to wave good-bye. Ten minutes later we were high over the Thames. I was really very sad. I have had such a wonderful year in England and have taken with me so many happy memories. My English has become fluent and my accent, I think, nearly perfect. I have made lots of good friends and learned a new way of life. I must come back soon.

Step 5

1 We needn't say good-bye now

Carsten and Jill are talking at the airport.
Here are Carsten's answers. What were Jill's questions?

Carsten: No, we needn't say good-bye now.   *Jill:* Must we say good-bye now?

We needn't walk up to the Roof Gardens.   *Jill:* .....
We needn't stay here much longer.   *Jill:* .....
We needn't leave the airport for our tea.   *Jill:* .....
Yes, I want to buy some picture-postcards.   *Jill:* .....
Yes, I want to take something English for our friends. *Jill:* .....
Yes, you can come over and visit us.   *Jill:* .....
Of course you can have our telephone number.   *Jill:* .....
Of course you may write to me often.   *Jill:* .....

2 Carsten explains

Carsten: We arrived much too early.
Sabine: We had lots of time.
Carsten: As we arrived much too early, we had lots of time.
Carsten: The Roof Gardens are open to visitors.
Sabine: We went up.
Carsten: As .....
Carsten: We haven't got much luggage.
Sabine: We can go up the escalator.
Carsten: As .....
Carsten: All seats on German planes were booked.
Sabine: We are going by British European Airways.
Carsten: As .....
Carsten: Many animals need a rest.
Sabine: They have opened an animal hotel.
Carsten: As .....
Carsten: We were thirsty.
Sabine: We all went to the airport cafeteria.
Carsten: As .....

3 Which is the quicker way?

Going by plane or going by boat? Going by plane is quicker than going by boat.
By express train or by car?
By car or by bike?
By bike or on foot?
By plane or by train?
By bike or by motor-bike?
By helicopter or by airliner?

4 Carsten didn't remember to thank me

Carsten left England. He didn't have a last cup of tea.
Carsten left England **without having a** last cup of tea.
Carsten left the airport. He didn't buy a postcard. Carsten left . . . . .
Carsten walked out of the school. He didn't take his books.
Carsten said good-bye to his mother. He didn't kiss her.
Carsten went out to the plane. He didn't wave.
Carsten sat down in the plane. He didn't fasten his seat-belt.
Carsten ate most of my strawberries. He didn't thank me.
Carsten slept for over an hour. He didn't read one page of his book.
Carsten arrived in Cologne. He didn't wake up.

5 A plane is on fire

Please read the story about the plane which is on fire on page 160. Then write the story again. Start: Last Wednesday I went to London Airport. I went up to the Roof Gardens. It was marvellous there. I was able to watch . . . I saw . . . Then a British European Airways jet started to . . . A television reporter beside me said: "..." I saw ambulances . . . I had a very good . . . Later I went to the cafeteria. There I saw the great film star . . . I wasn't able to see her face as . . . The television reporter asked her "..." She answered, "..." She asked a waitress for . . . It was a most exciting day.

6 Don't throw it away!

Please write a story about these pictures and use these words:

a) Last autumn Mr. Dinsdale started digging in his garden. Suddenly, to find, an awful, dirty old jug.
b) to throw, into the garden, neighbour, whom, to hate.
c) Neighbour, Mr. Robinson, a man, who, to love, old things. To take the jug into the kitchen, to wash it.

Unit 17

165

d) Mr. Robinson, to look at the clean jug. It is gold, very beautiful. To laugh and to show it, to stupid neighbour. Neighbour, to be very angry. To want to have the jug back. To say no and to say sorry.

e) Mr. Robinson, to go, to an antiques shop. Owner, to say, what a beautiful old jug. To ask, do you want to sell it to me? How much, to want? Not to know. Owner to give Mr. Robinson £ 350. Mr. Robinson to rush home and tell his wife.

7   Pattern Practice

Teacher: *Pupils:*

All seats on the plane were booked.

Teacher	Pupils
in the restaurant.	All seats in the restaurant were booked.
in the cinema.	All seats in the cinema were booked.
all beds in the hotel.	All beds in the hotel were booked.
on the ship.	All beds on the ship were booked.
all cabins.	All cabins on the ship were booked.
were free.	All cabins on the ship were free.

Stop. Now we begin a new drill.

We waited at the airport all morning.

Teacher	Pupils
all afternoon.	We waited at the airport all afternoon.
all evening.	We waited at the airport all evening.
on the Roof Gardens.	We waited on the Roof Gardens all evening.
all day.	We waited on the Roof Gardens all day.
We waited for a free seat.	We waited for a free seat all day.
all last month.	We waited for a free seat all last month.
a free cabin.	We waited for a free cabin all last month.
all July.	We waited for a free cabin all July.

8 Can you choose correctly: *although* or *because*?

Examples: I was sad **because** the weather was so awful.
The passengers waited all day **although** the weather forecast was excellent.

Write six sentences, please.

I The passengers The pilot The stewardess The announcer The airport porters	was sad waited all day took off fastened our seat belts announced the departure hurried up the escalator were fed up	because although	the weather was so awful we didn't like leaving London. it is better to be safe and sound. a storm was coming. there was lots of time. the jet to Rome was ready to leave. the weather forecast was excellent. we were to return to Germany.

9 Aural comprehension and composition: Goldie ■

10 In Selfridge's Department Store ★

11 A proverb: If at first you don't succeed, try, try again.

12 Sabine's English phrase-book

> There were <u>no fewer than</u> twenty girls at Angela's party and quite a few boys. Few of my own friends were there, but <u>a good few</u> of Carsten's girl-friends. Unfortunately the sandwiches were rather tasteless, and the cakes were <u>much the same</u>.

Unit 17　　　　　　　　　　　　　　　　　　　　　　167

13 Pairs

Can you complete these pairs?
We write these words differently, but we pronounce them in the same way:

Example: four — for   two — .....
         our — .....   their — .....
         sun — .....   know — .....
         sum — .....   meet — .....

14 The [ə:]-sound and the [ei] sound

Can you write down a long list of words which have the [ə:] sound?

start with these words: **bird, third.** Now please go on. Have you finished already? Well, then make **a list** of words with the [ei] sound. Start with the word **date.** Now go on.

15 A vocabulary quiz-game

The first member of the **German team** asks the first member of the **English team:**

"I'm afraid I'm a stranger here. Can you translate the word "opposite" into German for me?"

The member of the English team then answers with "Yes, I can" or "Sorry, I'm afraid I don't know" and says the German word, if he can. If he can't, his team gets a penalty point. Then the second member of the German team asks the second member of the English team: "I'm afraid I'm a stranger here. Can you translate the words 'auf Urlaub' into English for me?" Go on.

16 A letter to Barbara: Can you translate for her? ★

Appendix: An English Christmas

Christmas in England is a time for sending Christmas cards to all your friends and relations. That is why, in the week before Christmas Day, over a hundred million letters, cards and parcels come through the post every day. Schoolchildren over the age of sixteen can work as postmen during this week. Sometimes they find it very difficult to read the addresses. Quite often they find letters from small children with the address: "Father Christmas, Lapland"!

Two or three days before Christmas, the children help their mother to decorate the rooms with holly. They put it in vases, and on the tops of doors and pictures. Then they hang mistletoe on a lamp or just inside the front-door. You may kiss anyone you like, if he, or she, stands under the mistletoe. Most English people now also have a Christmas tree with candles and a star on top.

Christmas is a time for eating mince pies. Here is how you can make them: Put half a pound of flour into a bowl. Mix a quarter of a pound of butter and the flour with your fingers. Then add a little water, and mix. That is your pastry. Now you need nine small baking tins, a glass of mincemeat and the white of an egg. Mincemeat is made of apples, currants, raisins and spices. Next you roll the pastry, cut out nine rounds for the nine tins. Then you roll the rest of the pastry and cut out nine larger rounds. You put them into the tins, fill them with mincemeat, wet the edges and close the pies with the smaller rounds. Brush the tops with white of egg and put some fine sugar on top. Make two cuts in each top, then put the pies in a hot oven and bake them for half an hour. Eat them while they are still hot. Delicious!

Christmas is also a time for carol-singing. Here is an old English carol:

A Carol: I saw three ships

I saw three ships come sail-ing by, sail-ing by, sail-ing by, I saw three ships come sail-ing by, On Christ-mas Day in the morn-ing.

And what was in those ships all three,
On Christmas Day, on Christmas Day?
And what was in those ships all three
On Christmas Day in the morning?

Our Saviour Christ and his lady,
On Christmas Day, on Christmas Day.
Our Saviour Christ and his lady
On Christmas Day in the morning.

Here are the answers to the competition on page 147.

   a) false b) true c) true d) false e) false f) false g) true h) false i) false j) true